How to Master
Nursing
Calculations

2nd edition

Improve your maths
and make sense of
drug dosage charts

Chris
Tyreman

KoganPage

LONDON PHILADELPHIA NEW DELHI

While the author has made every effort to ensure that the content of this book is accurate, please note that occasional errors can occur in books of this kind. If you suspect that an error has been made in any of the tests included in this book, please inform the publisher at the address below so that it can be corrected at the next reprint.

Publisher's note
Every possible effort has been made to ensure that the information contained in this book is accurate at the time of going to press, and the publishers and author cannot accept responsibility for any errors or omissions, however caused. No responsibility for loss or damage occasioned to any person acting, or refraining from action, as a result of the material in this publication can be accepted by the editor, the publisher or the author.

First published in Great Britain in 2008 by Kogan Page Limited
Reissued 2010
Second edition 2013
Reprinted 2013 (twice), 2014 (three times), 2015 (three times)

2nd Floor, 45 Gee Street	1518 Walnut Street, Suite 1100	4737/23 Ansari Road
London, EC1V 3RS	Philadelphia PA 19102	Daryaganj
United Kingdom	USA	New Delhi 110002
www.koganpage.com		India

© Chris Tyreman, 2008, 2010, 2013

The right of Chris Tyreman to be identified as the author of this work has been asserted by him in accordance with the Copyright, Designs and Patents Act 1988.

British Library Cataloguing-in-Publication Data

A CIP record for this book is available from the British Library.

ISBN   978 0 7494 6753 1
E-ISBN 978 0 7494 6754 8

Typeset by Graphicraft Limited, Hong Kong
Printed and bound by Ashford Colour Press Ltd.

Unless you try to do something beyond what you have already mastered, you will never grow.

RALPH WALDO EMERSON 1803–1882

Contents

Introduction

Most medications are administered by nurses. Consequently it is nurses who are responsible for most of the errors made in drug administration. One source of mistakes is a lack of competence in drug dosage calculations. To promote safe practice, nursing schools can test for poor basic arithmetic skills both at the interview stage and during the three years of nurse training. This book teaches the skills necessary for success in these tests. It also explains how to read the drug treatment sheets used in the administration of medicines.

The mathematics knowledge required either at the interview stage or at nursing school does not exceed GCSE standard. You need only the four arithmetic skills of addition (+), subtraction (−), multiplication (×) and division (÷) as applied to whole numbers, fractions and decimal numbers. Knowledge of drug administration is not required for interview-type questions. Tests for student nurses may include medical terms and abbreviations, many of which are obvious, although a few Latin ones need to be remembered. This book does not cover all of the ones you will come across in nursing, only those that you are likely to meet in maths exams.

The book caters for most levels of mathematical ability, so it is suitable for mature students who have had little experience of numerical work since leaving school. Even candidates with very poor numerical skills should find it helpful.

Calculators are not allowed in the examination room, so it is vital that you can understand basic arithmetic processes and solve problems 'in you head' using mental arithmetic or by writing the calculation down on paper.

The first two chapters will familiarize you with the key topics of arithmetic, fractions, decimals and percentages. Chapter 3 introduces the metric system of measurement as appropriate to nursing. Chapter 4 covers drug dosage calculations, starting with simple problems that require only one or two arithmetic steps before moving on to more complicated calculations that require several arithmetic steps.

Chapter 5 covers drug names and drug dosage charts, or treatment sheets as they are known. It tests your ability to dispense the right drug in the right amount to the right patient via the right route at the right time – the five Rs of drug administration. It is not intended to test your knowledge of drugs, only your ability to read charts and carry out simple mathematical calculations. In practice you will need to reflect on normal doses, the purpose of the medication (its indication), unwanted side-effects and adverse reactions. These skills are essential for the safe administration of medications but are not part of this book.

The student is advised to work systematically through the book from start to finish, completing the in-text questions. The answers are to be found at the end of the book. If any chapter is too simple or does not meet your learning needs, then skip to the questions at the end of the chapter. If you can answer all of the questions correctly, you already have the essential knowledge and can move on to the next chapter.

The final chapter of the book contains practice questions of the type normally found in nursing school maths tests. A basic numerical test is followed by three nursing calculation mock tests of 50 questions each. You have one hour to complete each of the mock tests and the pass mark is 40 correct answers (80 per cent). Pass marks in nursing school tests are normally set high. Errors in drug administration are unacceptable and always require further investigation. When you are out on the wards the pass mark is 100 per cent!

Basic maths self-assessment test

Student nurses come from very varied backgrounds and have different employment and education experiences. The following test is aimed at students making a fresh start in education. It will reveal any gaps in your mathematical knowledge. There are three levels of difficulty: remedial, level 1 and level 2, with 10 questions at each level. If you make any mistakes at the remedial level, you may have a 'special needs' problem that is beyond the scope of this book. However, you should study the first eight pages of Chapter 1 and attempt the first two exercises before seeking help.

University students should be able to answer all of the questions at level 1 correctly. Wrong answers at this stage can be rectified by studying the first three chapters. Success at level 2 requires a firm foundation in numeracy. Mistakes made at this level will help you to identify those topics that need particular attention: for example, fractions, decimals, percentages or the metric system. Competency in these skills is essential for drug dosage calculations.

The test has no time limit nor does it require any knowledge of drug administration; calculators are not allowed. Answers can be found at the end of the book. There is no 'pass' mark but you can check your results against the following guide to numerical competency:

- Fewer than 10 correct answers: you may have numerical difficulties that require remedial help.

- 10 to 14 marks: you can recognize numbers and count but have problems with simple arithmetic problems.

- 15 to 20 marks: you have a grasp of basic arithmetic but have little knowledge of fractions, decimals or percentages.

- 21 to 25 marks: you have competent number skills but these could be extended further.

- 26 to 30 marks: you possess most of the basic skills necessary for success in drug dosage calculations.

Remedial

1   Write out 25 in words.
2   Write out 4060 in words.
3   Write out 980 107 in words.
4   Write out three thousand and thirty in figures.
5   Write out one million two hundred and ten thousand in figures.
6   Here are two numbers: 4900 and 12 500. Which is the larger?
7   Here are two numbers: 0.3 and 0.09. Which is the larger?
8   What does the 2 mean in 7250?
9   How many pence is £0.75?
10 If it is 8.30 pm now, what time will it be in 3 hours?

Level 1

11 $7 + 9 + 4 =$
12 $957 + 63 =$
13 $212 - 76 =$
14 $32 \times 9 =$
15 $315 \div 5 =$
16 How many more than 27 is 42?
17 What change should be handed over when a bill of £16.23 is paid with a £20 note?
18 Overnight the temperature rose from −1 °C to +4 °C. By how many degrees did it rise?
19 On average, a salesperson drives 450 miles per week. How many miles are driven per annum?
20 A lottery syndicate wins £225 000. If there are 20 people in the syndicate, how much will each person receive?

Level 2

21 $5\frac{1}{2} + 2\frac{1}{4} =$
22 $1\frac{2}{3} \div \frac{5}{9} =$
23 $8.2 + 7.45 =$
24 $4.5 \times 6 =$
25 $38 \div 0.5 =$
26 Find the interest paid on £8500 borrowed for 1 year at an interest rate of 12 per cent per annum.
27 Write 20% as a fraction.
28 Write 45% as a decimal.
29 How many milligrams are there in 0.25 grams?
30 Write 1.455 corrected to two decimal places.

23-38

Basic arithmetic skills

How to add, subtract, multiply and divide whole numbers

This first chapter is a refresher course in the basic arithmetic skills required for any mathematics test. If you find it too easy you can skip directly to the end-of-chapter questions. However, if you get any of the answers wrong you may have a numeracy problem that requires remedial help.

Numbers and place value

Starting at the simplest level, our number system is easily understood if you consider 'place value' where each number from 0 to 9 is written in a column – units, tens, hundreds and so on.

Numbers in words	Numbers in figures			
	Thou.	Hun.	Tens	Units
one hundred and seven	–	1	0	7
seven thousand two hundred	7	2	0	0
twenty five	–	–	2	5

Addition

Numbers to be added must be arranged underneath each other so that the unit columns are in line.

Example: 139 + 226
The first step is to align the numbers in columns.

$$
\begin{array}{c|c|c}
1 & 3 & 9 \\
2 & 2 & 6 \; +
\end{array}
$$

Then we add the units column (right-hand column)   6 + 9 = 15.
   The 5 is placed in the units column and the 10 carried over as one 'ten' into the tens column.

$$
\begin{array}{r}
1\;3\;9 \\
2\;2\;6 \; + \\
\hline
5 \\
\scriptstyle 1
\end{array}
$$

Now we add the tens column (middle column) remembering to include the 1 that has been carried:
   1 + 2 + 3 = 6 (middle column):

$$
\begin{array}{r}
1\;3\;9 \\
2\;2\;6 \; + \\
\hline
6\;5 \\
\scriptstyle 1
\end{array}
$$

Now we add the hundreds column: 2 + 1 = 3 (left-hand column).

$$
\begin{array}{r}
1\;3\;9 \\
2\;2\;6 \; + \\
\hline
3\;6\;5 \\
\scriptstyle 1
\end{array}
$$

For the addition of three or more numbers, the method is the same.

Example: 200 + 86 + 44 becomes:

```
  2 0 0
    8 6
    4 4 +
  -------
  3 3 0
  -------
  1 1
```

Subtraction

Subtraction is concerned with taking things away. Subtraction is the reverse of addition. The most important thing about subtraction is that the larger number is on top (above the smaller), so when subtracting numbers you *subtract the smaller number from the bigger number*.

As with addition, the numbers must be arranged underneath each other, so that the units columns are in line. After aligning the numbers, we subtract (take away) the columns vertically, starting at the right-hand end (units column).

For example: 374 – 126

```
3 | 7 | 4
1 | 2 | 6  –
```

The first step is to align the numbers:

The next step is to subtract the units column (the right-hand column): but 4 – 6 we cannot do since 6 is larger than 4. To overcome this problem we borrow 1 from the tens column (this is the same as 10 units) and add it to the 4 in the units column. So our sum now becomes:

14 – 6 (which we can do) = 8

So far we can write:

```
  3 7 ¹4
  1 2  6 –
  --------
        8
  --------
```

The next step is to pay back the '1' we have just borrowed from the tens column. There are two methods for doing this and both are now explained.

Method 1 (old-fashioned method – most popular)

In this method the 10 is paid back to the bottom, for example:

$$
\begin{array}{r}
3\ 7\ {}^{1}4 \\
1\ 2_1\ 6\ - \\
\hline
8 \\
\end{array}
$$

Now we add the 1 and the 2 to make 3. The 3 is subtracted from the 7 to give to the 4. So the sum becomes:

$$
\begin{array}{r}
3\ 7\ {}^{1}4 \\
1\ 2_1\ 6\ - \\
\hline
4\ \ 8 \\
\end{array}
$$

Finally we subtract the 1 from 3 (in the hundreds column) to give 2:

$$
\begin{array}{r}
3\ 7\ {}^{1}4 \\
1\ 2_1\ 6\ - \\
\hline
2\ 4\ \ 8 \\
\end{array}
$$

Method 2 (modern method)

In this method the 10 borrowed is subtracted as a 1 at the top of the tens column $(7 - 1 = 6)$, so:

$$
\begin{array}{r}
3\ 7^{6}14 \\
1\ 2_1\ 6\ - \\
\hline
2\ 4\ \ 8 \\
\end{array}
$$

Now try the following questions. *You must not use a calculator* for any questions in this book. Try to work out the answer 'in your head' if possible, otherwise do your working out on a separate sheet of paper.

Test 1

Write out the following numbers in figures:

1   one thousand one hundred and sixty eight.
2   nine thousand and forty two.
3   two thousand and nine.
4   twenty seven thousand five hundred and fifty.

Work out the following additions and subtractions:

5 $409 + 24 =$
6 $250 + 17\ 800 =$
7 $1427 - 300 =$
8 $6742 - 5630 =$

If any of your answers are wrong in Test 1 you may have a numeracy problem that requires remedial help.

Multiplication

Multiplication (or 'times') means 'lots of', and is a quick way of adding up numbers that have an equal value.

For example: 5 multiplied by $3 = 5 + 5 + 5$.

Note that $5 \times 3 = 15$ and $3 \times 5 = 15$.

This applies to all numbers that are multiplied together: it does not matter which way around you put them, the answer is the same.

To work with multiplication sums you need to be familiar with your 'times tables'. The most common times tables are shown in Table 1.2. It is essential that you memorize these tables because calculators are not allowed in the examination room.

The multiplication table in Table 1.1 is a handy way of finding the answer (known as the 'product') when any two numbers from 0 to 12 are multiplied together. See whether you can find out how to use it – it's not difficult!

Short multiplication

This is the term for the multiplication of any number by a unit (1 to 9).

TABLE 1.1 Multiplication table (try to memorize it)

	1	2	3	4	5	6	7	8	9	10	11	12
1	1	2	3	4	5	6	7	8	9	10	11	12
2	2	4	6	8	10	12	14	16	18	20	22	24
3	3	6	9	12	15	18	21	24	27	30	33	36
4	4	8	12	16	20	24	28	32	36	40	44	48
5	5	10	15	20	25	30	35	40	45	50	55	60
6	6	12	18	24	30	36	42	48	54	60	66	72
7	7	14	21	28	35	42	49	56	63	70	77	84
8	8	16	24	32	40	48	56	64	72	80	88	96
9	9	18	27	36	45	54	63	72	81	90	99	108
10	10	20	30	40	50	60	70	80	90	100	110	120
11	11	22	33	44	55	66	77	88	99	110	121	132
12	12	24	36	48	60	72	84	96	108	120	132	144

Examples are:

$$3 \times 8$$
$$3\,2 \times 4$$
$$1\,0\,8 \times 9$$
$$5\,2\,4 \times 3$$

↑ All units

For example: 19×3. We write the sum as:

$$1\,9$$
$$3 \times$$

First we multiply the 9 by the 3 to give 27:

$9 \times 3 = 27$ (see three times table).

As with addition the 7 is written in the units column and the 2 is carried as two tens into the tens column as follows:

$$1\,9$$
$$\underline{3 \times}$$
$$\underline{7}$$
$$2$$

TABLE 1.2 The common times tables

2 times	3 times	4 times	5 times	6 times	7 times
1×2 = 2	1×3 = 3	1×4 = 4	1×5 = 5	1×6 = 6	1×7 = 7
2×2 = 4	2×3 = 6	2×4 = 8	2×5 = 10	2×6 = 12	2×7 = 14
3×2 = 6	3×3 = 9	3×4 = 12	3×5 = 15	3×6 = 18	3×7 = 21
4×2 = 8	4×3 = 12	4×4 = 16	4×5 = 20	4×6 = 24	4×7 = 28
5×2 = 10	5×3 = 15	5×4 = 20	5×5 = 25	5×6 = 30	5×7 = 35
6×2 = 12	6×3 = 18	6×4 = 24	6×5 = 30	6×6 = 36	6×7 = 42
7×2 = 14	7×3 = 21	7×4 = 28	7×5 = 35	7×6 = 42	7×7 = 49
8×2 = 16	8×3 = 24	8×4 = 32	8×5 = 40	8×6 = 48	8×7 = 56
9×2 = 18	9×3 = 27	9×4 = 36	9×5 = 45	9×6 = 54	9×7 = 63
10×2 = 20	10×3 = 30	10×4 = 40	10×5 = 50	10×6 = 60	10×7 = 70
11×2 = 22	11×3 = 33	11×4 = 44	11×5 = 55	11×6 = 66	11×7 = 77
12×2 = 24	12×3 = 36	12×4 = 48	12×5 = 60	12×6 = 72	12×7 = 84

8 times	9 times	10 times	11 times	12 times
1×8 = 8	1×9 = 9	1×10 = 10	1×11 = 11	1×12 = 12
2×8 = 16	2×9 = 18	2×10 = 20	2×11 = 22	2×12 = 24
3×8 = 24	3×9 = 27	3×10 = 30	3×11 = 33	3×12 = 36
4×8 = 32	4×9 = 36	4×10 = 40	4×11 = 44	4×12 = 48
5×8 = 40	5×9 = 45	5×10 = 50	5×11 = 55	5×12 = 60
6×8 = 48	6×9 = 54	6×10 = 60	6×11 = 66	6×12 = 72
7×8 = 56	7×9 = 63	7×10 = 70	7×11 = 77	7×12 = 84
8×8 = 64	8×9 = 72	8×10 = 80	8×11 = 88	8×12 = 96
9×8 = 72	9×9 = 81	9×10 = 90	9×11 = 99	9×12 = 108
10×8 = 80	10×9 = 90	10×10 = 100	10×11 = 110	10×12 = 120
11×8 = 88	11×9 = 99	11×10 = 110	11×11 = 121	11×12 = 132
12×8 = 96	12×9 = 108	12×10 = 120	12×11 = 132	12×12 = 144

Now we multiply the 1 by the 3 to give 3 ($1 \times 3 = 3$). This 3 is added to the 2 previously carried to the tens column to give 5, so the finished sum becomes:

$$
\begin{array}{r}
1\ 9 \\
3 \times \\
\hline
5\ 7 \\
\hline
2 \hphantom{\ 0}
\end{array}
$$

so $19 \times 3 = 57$.

Example: what is 68×9? We rewrite the sum as:

$$
\begin{array}{r}
6\ 8 \\
9 \times
\end{array}
$$

Multiplying the units gives $8 \times 9 = 72$ (see nine times table), so we have:

$$
\begin{array}{r}
6\ 8 \\
9 \times \\
\hline
2 \\
\hline
7 \hphantom{\ 0}
\end{array}
$$

We multiply the 6 in the tens column by the 9 to give $6 \times 9 = 54$. The 54 is added to the 7 previously carried, to give $54 + 7 = 61$. The 1 of the 61 is placed in the tens column and the 6 of the 61 is carried into the hundreds column:

$$
\begin{array}{r}
6\ 8 \\
9 \times \\
\hline
1\ 2 \\
\hline
6\ 7 \hphantom{\ 0}
\end{array}
$$

Since there are no hundreds to multiply in the hundreds column, the figure 6 can be carried directly into this column, giving:

$$
\begin{array}{r}
6\ 8 \\
9 \times \\
\hline
6\ 1\ 2 \\
\hline
6\ 7 \hphantom{\ 0}
\end{array}
$$

Test 2

Calculate the following multiplication sums:

1 7×9
2 12×8
3   Multiply 20 by 6.
4   Multiply 23 by 4.
5   90 times 5 is ...
6   The product of 19 and 5 is ...
7 $33 \times 3 = ...$
8 $75 \times 4 = ...$
9 $125 \times 8 = ...$
10 $11 \times 12 = ...$

Long multiplication

This is the term for multiplying any number by a number greater than 9, for example 52×18 or 120×50.

To multiply 52×18 we rewrite this as:

$$
\begin{array}{r}
5\,2 \\
1\,8 \times \\
\hline
\\
\hline
\end{array}
$$

We proceed in two steps as follows. First we multiply the 52 by the 8 in the units column and second we multiply the 52 by the 1 in the tens column.

First step: (multiply 52 by the 8) so we have:

$$
\begin{array}{r}
5\,2 \\
1\,8 \times \\
\hline
4\,1\,6 \\
\scriptstyle 1
\end{array}
$$

Second step (multiply the 52 by the 1 in the tens column). Since we are now multiplying from the tens column we leave the units column blank, which is the same as filling it with a 0. The sum is written on the line below 416:

$$
\begin{array}{r}
5\ 2 \\
\underline{1\ 8} \times \\
4\ 1\ 6 \\
\underline{5\ 2\ 0}
\end{array}
$$

We now add the two steps together: add 416 and 520 to give the final sum which is shown below:

$$
\begin{array}{r}
5\ 2 \\
\underline{1\ 8} \times \\
4\ 1\ 6 \\
\underline{5\ 2\ 0} \\
\underline{9\ 3\ 6}
\end{array}
$$

Test 3

Work out the following multiplication sums:

1	62 × 13	**6**	125 × 80
2	79 × 32	**7**	167 × 33
3	80 × 15	**8**	42 × 121
4	254 × 20	**9**	195 × 205
5	17 × 25	**10**	13 × 54

Division

Division is the reverse of multiplication, and is concerned with sharing (or dividing numbers into equal parts).

Example: divide 195 by 3. So we have 195 ÷ 3 which is rewritten

$$3\overline{)1\ 9\ 5}$$

The first step is to divide the 1 by the 3. However, since 3 into 1 won't go, we have to carry the 1 into the next column, so:

$$3\overline{)1\ ^19\ 5}$$

We now use the multiplication table in reverse to find how many 3s are in 19. To do this start in the 3s column on the left-hand side and move along the horizontal row until you get to the number that is closest to but smaller than 19. The number is 18. Following the vertical row upwards gives us 6. So 3 goes into 19 six times with 1 left over (19 − 18 = 1 left over). The 6 is placed at the top; the 1 is carried to the next column to make 15.

$$\frac{6}{3\overline{)1\ ^19\ ^15}}$$

Finally the 3 is divided into 15. The three times table shows us that 3 goes into 15 times exactly, so the finished sum is:

$$\frac{6\ \ 5}{3\overline{)1\ ^19\ ^15}}$$

The answer can be checked by multiplying it by the number that we have divided by (65 × 3 = 195: correct).

Test 4

Work out the following divisions:

1	36 ÷ 9	**5**	1230 ÷ 3
2	248 ÷ 4	**6**	295 ÷ 5
3	3⟌339	**7**	1464 ÷ 6
4	5⟌265	**8**	1000 ÷ 8

Long division

This is the term for division by large numbers.

Example: for 2064 divided by 48 we write: $48\overline{)2064}$
First step: divide 2 by 48 – won't go
Second step: divide 20 by 48 – won't go
Third step: divide 206 by 48 – will go
48 into 206 will go, but we don't have a times table for 48 so we have
to *build up a table ourselves*. This is done as follows:

$1 \times 48 = 48$
$2 \times 48 = 96$
$3 \times 48 = 144$
$4 \times 48 = 192$ (the nearest to 206)
$5 \times 48 = 240$ (too big)

Fourth step: work out the remainder. We know that 48 goes into 206
four times to leave a remainder of 14 (206 – 192 = 14).

```
              4
    4 8 | 2 0 6 4
        | 1 9 2 –
        ─────────
            1 4
```

Fifth step: we now bring the 4 down to give 144:

```
              4
    4 8 | 2 0 6 4
        | 1 9 2 –
        ─────────
            1 4 4
```

Sixth step: the 48 is divided into 144 to give 3 with no remainder
(see 48 times table on page 17).

```
            4 3
    4 8 | 2 0 6 4
        | 1 9 2 –
        ─────────
            1 4 4
            1 4 4 –
```

So, 2064 ÷ 48 = 43.

Test 5

Work out the following long division sums:

1	360 ÷ 12	**6**	216 ÷ 36
2	372 ÷ 12	**7**	950 ÷ 25
3	18⟌792	**8**	2680 ÷ 40
4	20⟌900	**9**	976 ÷ 16
5	72⟌1440	**10**	4944 ÷ 24

By now you should be familiar with the four basic rules of arithmetic: that is, how to add, subtract, multiply and divide whole numbers. The next chapter explains how to use these maths skills with fractions and decimals.

Sequence of operations ('BoDMAS')

A calculation with two or more arithmetic signs (or operations) must be worked out in the correct sequence, which is:

Multiplication and division before addition and subtraction.

Example: $4 \times 3 + 6$

Multiplication first: $4 \times 3 = 12$ followed by addition: $12 + 6 = 18$
So $4 \times 3 + 6 = 18$

If we carried out the addition part first ($3 + 6 = 9$) and then multiplied by the 4 this would have given 36 ($4 \times 9 = 36$), which is the wrong answer.

Example: $25 - 12 \div 3$

Division first: $12 \div 3 = 4$ followed by subtraction $25 - 4 = 21$
So $25 - 12 \div 3 = 21$

Where a calculation contains only addition and subtraction, each part is worked out in a sequence from left to right.

Example: 11 – 3 + 9 – 2 becomes 11 – 3 = 8 then 8 + 9 = 17 then finally 17 – 2 = 15

Where a calculation contains only multiplication and division, each part out is worked out in sequence from left to right.

Example: 10 ÷ 2 × 6 becomes 10 ÷ 2 = 5 followed by 5 × 6 = 30

Test 6

Work out the following (without using a calculator):

1	12 ÷ 6 + 12	**7**	14 + 11 – 10 – 6 =
2	10 + 15 ÷ 5	**8**	22 × 4 ÷ 2 + 12 =
3	3 × 4 – 2	**9**	30 ÷ 6 × 5 – 15 =
4	8 – 3 × 2	**10**	2 × 3 × 4 × 5 ÷ 20 =
5	10 + 20 ÷ 5	**11**	10 – 1 × 3 – 1 =
6	15 – 9 + 3	**12**	9 + 3 × 4 ÷ 2 – 1 =

Some calculations include brackets to help make sure that the arithmetic is carried out in the correct sequence. Where a calculation contains brackets, the sum inside the brackets must be worked out first.

Example: 12 ÷ (6 – 2)
First step: (6 – 2) = 4
Second step 12 ÷ 4 = 3
So 12 ÷ (6 – 2) = 3

Without the brackets, 12 ÷ 6 – 2 is 12 ÷ 6 = 2, then 2 – 2 = 0.

You can remember the sequence of operations as **BoDMAS**: **B**rackets, **D**ivision, **M**ultiplication, **A**ddition and **S**ubtraction.

Finally, you should be aware that when no arithmetic sign is placed outside the brackets, the calculation is automatically taken as being times (×). This rule applies to every calculation where there is no sign outside the bracket. So 9(6 + 5) means 9 × (6 + 5) and the sum becomes 9 × 11 = 99.

Test 7

Calculate the following by working out the brackets first:

1	9 + (5 × 3)	**7**	3(10 + 6 ÷ 2)
2	14 − (10 + 2)	**8**	3 + 6(4 × 2 + 1)
3	30 ÷ (3 × 2)	**9**	2(23 − 17) ÷ 4
4	4 × (20 − 9)	**10**	4 + 4(4 + 4)
5	10(10 − 9)	**11**	90 ÷ 9(8 − 3 × 2)
6	7(15 ÷ 5)	**12**	10 × 2(60 ÷ 2 × 15)

Factors and multiples

Skill with numbers will help you to work out drug dosage calculations without having to use a calculator. The ability to break down large numbers is an essential part of working with fractions. The latter form the basis of many drug calculations.

Factors are numbers that will divide into another number exactly, without leaving a remainder. For example:

15 is a factor of 60 (60 divided by 15 = 4)
50 is a factor of 250 (250 divided by 50 = 5)
100 is a factor of 1000 (1000 divided by 100 = 10)

All the factors of a number are all of the whole numbers that will divide into it exactly. Take the number 36 for example. The factors of 36 are:

1 and 36
2 and 18
3 and 12
4 and 9
6 and 6

Notice how the factors are found in pairs. Pairing off in this way will help you to find the factors of large numbers, without missing any out. The factors of 36 can be listed as:

1 2 3 4 6 9 12 18 and 36.

The highest common factor (HCF) of two numbers is the highest of their common factors. For example: what is the highest common factor of 60 and 15?

15: factors = 1 3 5 15
60: factors = 1 2 3 4 5 6 10 12 15 20 30 60

The factors that are common to both 15 and 60 are 1, 3, 5 and 15, and of these 15 is the highest, so 15 is the HCF of 60 and 15.

Example: what is the HCF of 20 and 16?

16: 1 2 4 8 16
20: 1 2 4 5 10 20

1, 2 and 4 are the common factors so 4 is the HCF of 16 and 20.

Test 8

Find the factors of the following numbers. Use the pairing-off method (1 and; 2 and; 3 and; 4 and; 5 and; 6 and; etc):

1   6 (four factors)
2   10 (four factors)
3   32 (six factors)
4   90 (12 factors)
5   500 (12 factors)

Find the highest common factor (HCF) of:

6   24 and 32
7   75 and 120
8   12 and 500
9   50 and 1000
10   25 and 400

A *prime number* is a number that is only divisible by itself and 1. It has only two factors – the number itself and 1. The lowest prime number is 2 (1 is not a prime number because it has only one factor – itself).

All the prime numbers below 50 are listed below:

2 3 5 7 11 13 17 19 23 29 31 37 41 43 47

Note: with the exception of 2 all the prime numbers are odd numbers (but not all odd numbers are prime numbers).

A factor that is a prime number is called a *prime factor*. To find the prime factors of any number we keep dividing by prime numbers – starting with the lowest prime number that will divide into it, and then progressing through until it will not divide by any prime number any further.

Example: what are the prime factors of 210?

$$210 \div 2 = 105$$
$$105 \div 3 = 35$$
$$35 \div 5 = 7$$
$$7 \div 7 = 1$$

So 210 has the prime factors 2, 3, 5, and 7.

$$210 = 2 \times 3 \times 5 \times 7$$

Example: express 2520 as a product of its prime factors.
As in the previous example we start dividing by the lowest prime number, which is 2:

$$2520 \div 2 = 1260$$

1260 is an even number so it will divide by 2 again:

$$1260 \div 2 = 630$$

630 is an even number so it will divide by 2 again:

$$630 \div 2 = 315$$

315 is an odd number so it will not divide by 2 but it will divide by the next prime number which is 3:

$$315 \div 3 = 105$$

105 will divide by 3 again:

$$105 \div 3 = 35$$

35 will not divide by 3, but it will divide by the next prime number which is 5:

$35 \div 5 = 7$

7 is a prime number so it will not divide any further.

$7 \div 7 = 1$

So, $2520 = 2 \times 2 \times 2 \times 3 \times 3 \times 5 \times 7$.

Note: finding the correct prime factors involves trial and error if the number does not divide by the first prime factor you try.

$209 \div 2 = 104$ remainder 1, so 2 is not a prime factor of 209.
$209 \div 3 = 69$ remainder 2, so 3 is not a prime factor of 209.
$209 \div 5 = 41$ remainder 4, so 5 is not a prime factor of 209.
$209 \div 7 = 29$ remainder 6, so 7 is not a prime factor of 209.
$209 \div 11 = 19$ exactly so 11 is a prime factor of 209.

From this we can see that 209 has the prime factors 11 and 19.

Test 9

Express the following numbers as a product of their prime factors (2 3 5 7 11 13 etc):

1	6	**5**	81
2	30	**6**	216
3	63	**7**	125
4	420	**8**	343

A *multiple* of a number is the number multiplied by:

1 2 3 4 5 6 7 8 9 10 11 12 13 14 etc.

So a multiple is the 'times table' of a number. For example:

The multiples of 5 are: 5 10 15 20 25 30 etc.
The multiples of 6 are: 6 12 18 24 30 etc.
The multiples of 10 are: 10 20 30 40 50 etc.

Common multiples are those numbers that are common to a pair of numbers. For example, what are the first three common multiples of 5 and 10?

multiples of 5: 5 <u>10</u> 15 <u>20</u> 25 <u>30</u>
multiples of 10: <u>10</u> <u>20</u> <u>30</u> 40 50

The common numbers are underlined, so the first three common multiples of 5 and 10 are: 10, 20 and 30. The lowest of these is 10, making it the lowest common multiple (LCM); it is the lowest number that both 5 and 10 will divide into exactly.

Example: Find the lowest common multiple (LCM) of 3 and 9.

multiples of 3: 3 6 9 12 18
multiples of 9: 9 18 27 36 45
so the LCM of 3 and 9 is 9.

Example: Find the lowest common multiple (LCM) of 4 and 5.

4: 4 8 12 16 20 24
5: 5 10 15 20 25
so LCM is 20.

Test 10

Find the first four multiples of:

1 2
2 12
3 20
4 25
5 100

Find the lowest common multiple (LCM) of:

6 2 and 3
7 12 and 20
8 24 and 36
9 30 and 75
10 25 and 40

Chapter 1 questions

1 Write out two thousand and twenty two in figures.
2 Add 434 and 176.
3 Subtract 51 from 246.
4 Subtract 2750 from 5342.
5 Multiply 9 by 12.
6 Multiply 8 × 8.
7 Multiply 125 × 45.
8 Multiply 1053 × 141.
9 Divide 121 by 11.
10 Divide 195 by 5.
11 Divide 3136 by 14.
12 Divide 1728 by 24.
13 Divide 1040 by 8.
14 $10 + 20 \div 2 =$
15 $20 \div 2 \times 10 =$
16 $10 + 4 - 5 + 7 =$
17 $8 \times 3 \div 4 \times 9 =$
18 $10(5 + 3) =$
19 $2(8 + 10 \div 2) =$
20 $3 \times 5(12 \div 3 + 6) =$
21 Find the factors of 20.
22 What are the prime factors of 20?
23 Find the factors of 42.
24 What are the prime factors of 42?
25 Write down the first six multiples of 6.
26 Write down the first six multiples of 9.
27 What is the lowest common multiple of 6 and 9?
28 What is the lowest common multiple of 20 and 25?
29 What is the lowest common multiple of 50 and 250?
30 What is the lowest common multiple of 10 and 12?

Fractions and decimals

Introduction to fractions

We use fractions in everyday situations; for example, we talk about *half* an hour, *three-quarters* of a mile or shops selling goods with a discount of *one-third*.

$\frac{1}{2}$ hour $\frac{3}{4}$ mile $\frac{1}{3}$ discount

You will be familiar with these everyday examples of fractions. Each of these fractions consists of part of the whole, so they indicate part of an hour, part of a mile and part of the price.

So a fraction is: the whole divided into a number of equal parts.

All fractions have a top and bottom number. The bottom number, or *denominator*, tells us how many equal parts the whole is divided into. The top number, or *numerator*, tells us how many parts we have. So half an hour means that we divide the hour into two equal parts and we have one part.

An easy way to understand fractions is to draw the whole in diagram form and shade in the fraction. For example:

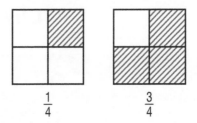

$$\frac{1}{4}$$ $$\frac{3}{4}$$

Cancelling (equivalent fractions)

Some fractions can be cancelled so as to express them in smaller numbers. The value of the fraction is not altered by cancelling and so the outcome is an *equivalent fraction*.

For example, *four-sixths* can be expressed as a fraction having smaller numbers, by dividing *both* the top and bottom numbers by 2. This is known as *cancelling*.

$$\frac{4\div2}{6\div2} = \frac{2}{3}$$

Remember, the value of the fraction has not become smaller, only the numbers involved – this means that *four-sixths* and *two-thirds* are equivalent fractions:

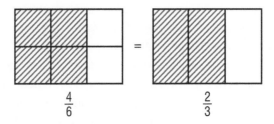

$$\frac{4}{6}$$ $$\frac{2}{3}$$

Another example of cancelling is $\frac{8}{16}$. This fraction can be cancelled three times as follows:

$\frac{8}{16}$ can be cancelled to $\frac{4}{8}$ by dividing the 8 and the 16 by 2.
$\frac{8}{16}$ can be cancelled to $\frac{2}{4}$ by dividing the 8 and the 16 by 4.
$\frac{8}{16}$ can be cancelled to $\frac{1}{2}$ by dividing the 8 and the 16 by 8.

So the equivalent fractions are $\frac{8}{16} = \frac{4}{8} = \frac{2}{4} = \frac{1}{2}$.

If we cancel $\frac{8}{16}$ to $\frac{1}{2}$ this is known as cancelling a fraction to its lowest terms (it cannot be reduced any further).

Test 11

Cancel the following fractions to their lowest terms (hints given):

1 $\frac{3}{6}$ (divide the top and the bottom by 3).
2 $\frac{15}{20}$ (divide the top and the bottom by 5).
3 $\frac{12}{36}$ (divide the top and bottom by 12, or by 2, 2, and 3).
4 $\frac{40}{72}$ (divide by the smallest prime number, three times over).
5 $\frac{16}{24}$ (try dividing by small prime numbers).
6 $\frac{18}{30}$ (try dividing by small prime numbers).
7 $\frac{10}{100}$ (numbers ending in zero always divide by 10).
8 $\frac{95}{100}$ (numbers ending in 5 always divide by 5).
9 $\frac{8}{12}$ (use the methods outlined above).
10 $\frac{40}{100}$ (use the methods outlined above).

How to add and subtract fractions

Addition and subtraction of fractions can be dealt with together as the same 'rules' apply to both. Multiplication and division of fractions have different rules and will be explained separately.

For us to be able to add or subtract fractions they must have the same denominators. Take the following example:

$$\frac{1}{8} + \frac{3}{8}$$

Both fractions have a denominator of 8. We write the denominator *once*, and then add the two top numbers:

$$\text{so } \frac{1}{8} + \frac{3}{8} = \frac{1+3}{8} = \frac{4}{8}$$

An example of subtraction is:

$$\frac{13}{16} - \frac{5}{16} = \frac{13-5}{16} = \frac{8}{16}$$

Test 12

Add/subtract the following fractions then cancel where possible (questions 5 to 8):

1	$\frac{6}{8} + \frac{1}{8}$		**5**	$\frac{7}{9} - \frac{2}{9} + \frac{4}{9}$
2	$\frac{2}{6} + \frac{3}{6}$		**6**	$\frac{11}{12} - \frac{5}{12}$
3	$\frac{7}{10} - \frac{4}{10}$		**7**	$\frac{9}{15} + \frac{1}{15}$
4	$\frac{11}{12} - \frac{4}{12}$		**8**	$\frac{12}{40} + \frac{4}{40}$

When the fractions have different denominators we can still add or subtract them, but in order to do so we first of all have to find a *common denominator*. This is a number that both denominators will divide into. Take the following example:

$$\frac{1}{4} + \frac{3}{6}$$

The first fraction has a denominator of 4 and the second fraction has a denominator of 6. The *common denominator* is a number that both 4 and 6 will divide into. There are many numbers that both 4 and 6 will divide into. To find them we compare the 4 times table with the 6 times table and see where they give us the same answer. From these tables, we can see that 4 and 6 have common denominators at 12, 24, 36 and 48. To make the working easier we choose the lowest of these, 12 (the lowest common factor as explained in Chapter 1).

4 times table	6 times table
1×4 = 4	1×6 = 6
2×4 = 8	2×6 = **12**
3×4 = **12**	3×6 = 18
4×4 = 16	4×6 = **24**
5×4 = 20	5×6 = 30
6×4 = **24**	6×6 = **36**
7×4 = 28	7×6 = 42
8×4 = 32	8×6 = **48**
9×4 = **36**	9×6 = 54
10×4 = 40	10×6 = 60
11×4 = 44	11×6 = 66
12×4 = **48**	12×6 = 72

The above tables show us that 12 is the lowest common denominator (LCD). To proceed with the sum, the next stage is to rewrite each fraction in terms of the common denominator, 12ths. So we rewrite $\frac{1}{4}$ in 12ths and $\frac{3}{6}$ in 12ths.

To do this we divide the common denominator 12 by the denominators of the two fractions (4 and 6 in the above example) and then multiply the numerator of each fraction by the respective answer.

We rewrite $\frac{1}{4}$ in 12ths as follows:

$12 \div 4 = 3$ (common denominator 12 ÷ denominator of 4 = 3)
$3 \times 1 = 3$ (answer 3 × numerator of 1 = 3)

So we have $\frac{1}{4} = \frac{3}{12}$. Similarly $\frac{3}{6}$ in 12ths is rewritten:

$12 \div 6 = 2$ (common denominator 12 ÷ denominator of 6 = 2)
$2 \times 3 = 6$ (answer 2 × numerator of 3 = 6)

So we have $\frac{3}{6} = \frac{6}{12}$.

The sum of $\frac{1}{4} + \frac{3}{6}$ now becomes: $\frac{3}{12} + \frac{6}{12}$. Since these fractions have the same denominator they can be added together as with the previous example:

$$\frac{3}{12} + \frac{6}{12} = \frac{3+6}{12} = \frac{9}{12}$$

Test 13

Work out the lowest common denominator (LCD) of:

1 $\frac{1}{5}$ and $\frac{4}{15}$
2 $\frac{1}{4}$ and $\frac{2}{3}$
3 $\frac{9}{16}$, $\frac{1}{8}$ and $\frac{3}{4}$

Calculate the following using the LCDs above:

4 $\frac{1}{5} + \frac{4}{15}$
5 $\frac{1}{4} + \frac{2}{3}$
6 $\frac{9}{16} - \frac{1}{8}$

Test 14

Work out the LCD and then *choose the larger fraction*. Try to work out the answers 'in your head' as far as possible.

1 $\frac{2}{3}$ $\frac{3}{4}$

2 $\frac{2}{3}$ $\frac{5}{9}$ $\frac{11}{18}$

3 $\frac{1}{3}$ $\frac{2}{5}$ $\frac{11}{30}$

4 $\frac{3}{4}$ $\frac{5}{6}$ $\frac{7}{8}$

5 $\frac{30}{100}$ $\frac{7}{25}$ $\frac{16}{50}$

6 $\frac{7}{100}$ $\frac{3}{50}$ $\frac{10}{1000}$

How to multiply and divide fractions

Multiplication is straightforward. All you have to do is multiply the two numerators (top numbers) together and multiply the two denominators (bottom numbers) together.

Example:

$$\frac{1}{5} \times \frac{2}{3} = \frac{1 \times 2}{5 \times 3} = \frac{2}{15}$$

So when multiplying fractions together the rule is:

Multiply the two top numbers
Multiply the two bottom numbers

Test 15

Calculate the following and cancel the answer where possible:

1 $\frac{2}{3} \times \frac{1}{9}$

2 $\frac{4}{15} \times \frac{2}{3}$

3 $\frac{4}{7} \times \frac{4}{9}$

4 $\frac{2}{3} \times \frac{1}{9}$

5 $\frac{3}{5} \times \frac{1}{100}$

6 $\frac{2}{3} \times \frac{3}{4}$

7 $\frac{3}{5} \times \frac{5}{9}$

8 $\frac{7}{20} \times \frac{5}{7}$

9 $\frac{2}{9} \times \frac{3}{9}$

10 $\frac{9}{10} \times \frac{1}{3}$

Division of fractions is similar except the fraction on the right-hand side must be:

● turned upside down (example: $\frac{3}{5}$ becomes $\frac{5}{3}$);
● then multiplied with the fraction on the left-hand side.

Example: $\frac{1}{5} \div \frac{3}{10} = ?$

Step one, $\frac{3}{10}$ becomes $\frac{10}{3}$

Step two, $\frac{1}{5} \times \frac{10}{3} = \frac{10}{15}$

So when dividing fractions the rule is:

Turn the right-hand fraction upside down and then multiply the two fractions together.

Test 16

Calculate the following divisions by turning the right-hand side fraction upside down before multiplying the two fractions together.

1	$\frac{1}{6} \div \frac{1}{4}$	**6**	$\frac{12}{100} \div \frac{3}{10}$
2	$\frac{1}{3} \div \frac{5}{9}$	**7**	$\frac{8}{1000} \div \frac{1}{5}$
3	$\frac{3}{16} \div \frac{1}{4}$	**8**	$\frac{1}{250} \div \frac{1}{5}$
4	$\frac{3}{10} \div \frac{3}{5}$	**9**	$\frac{2}{125} \div \frac{8}{75}$
5	$\frac{5}{12} \div \frac{1}{2}$	**10**	$\frac{3}{7} \div \frac{9}{14}$

Improper fractions

Until now, we have worked with fractions that have denominators greater than the numerator (bottom greater than top).

Examples are $\frac{1}{4}, \frac{5}{6}, \frac{9}{10}, \frac{13}{16}$ – these are known as *vulgar fractions*. However, some fractions are *top heavy*, as in $\frac{17}{6}, \frac{9}{4}$ and $\frac{65}{25}$. Here the numerator is greater than the denominator. These fractions are known as *improper fractions*, and are added, subtracted, multiplied and divided in the same way as for vulgar fractions.

Example: $\frac{5}{2} + \frac{7}{3} = \frac{15+14}{6} = \frac{29}{6}$

Example: $\frac{9}{5} - \frac{10}{6} = \frac{63-50}{35} = \frac{13}{35}$

Example: $\frac{9}{4} \times \frac{8}{5} = \frac{72}{20} = \frac{18}{5}$

Example: $\frac{11}{4} \div \frac{9}{7} = \frac{11}{4} \times \frac{7}{9} = \frac{77}{36}$

Test 17

Work out the following sums containing improper fractions, and cancel your answers where possible.

1	$\frac{7}{6} + \frac{11}{12}$	**5**	$\frac{12}{5} + \frac{5}{2}$
2	$\frac{14}{3} - \frac{9}{2}$	**6**	$\frac{5}{3} \times \frac{8}{5}$
3	$\frac{5}{4} \times \frac{3}{2}$	**7**	$\frac{25}{6} \div \frac{15}{8}$
4	$\frac{6}{5} \div \frac{12}{5}$	**8**	$\frac{75}{20} \times \frac{40}{3}$

Mixed fractions

A mixed fraction consists of a whole number with a vulgar fraction. Examples of mixed fractions are:

$$1\tfrac{1}{2}, 2\tfrac{5}{6}, 5\tfrac{1}{3}, 3\tfrac{3}{4}$$

To be able to work out sums containing mixed fractions we have to turn the mixed fraction into an improper fraction. To do this, we first separate the whole number from the vulgar fraction, for example:

$1\tfrac{1}{2}$ is one whole and one half: $1 + \tfrac{1}{2}$

The next step is to write the whole number in terms of the fraction. In the above example, 1 is 2 halves, so:

$1 = \tfrac{2}{2}$

We can now add the whole, expressed as a fraction, to the vulgar fraction:

$$1\tfrac{1}{2} = \tfrac{2}{2} + \tfrac{1}{2} = \tfrac{3}{2}$$

So $1\tfrac{1}{2}$ as an improper fraction is $\tfrac{3}{2}$.

Similarly, $2\tfrac{3}{4} = \tfrac{8}{4} + \tfrac{3}{4} = \tfrac{11}{4}$.

This example can also be shown in diagram form:

$$2\frac{3}{4} \quad = \quad \frac{11}{4}$$

A more mathematical way of converting a mixed fraction to an improper fraction is as follows:

Step 1: multiply the whole number by the denominator of the vulgar fraction.

Step 2: put the answer in step 1 over the denominator of the vulgar fraction.

Step 3: combine the vulgar fraction with the answer in step 2.

Example: write the mixed fraction $2\frac{1}{4}$ as an improper fraction.

Step 1: $2 \times 4 = 8$

Step 2: $\frac{8}{4}$ (2 wholes = 8 quarters)

Step 3: $\frac{8}{4} + \frac{1}{4} = \frac{9}{4}$

So $2\frac{1}{4}$ as an improper fraction is $\frac{9}{4}$.

Test 18

Convert the following mixed fractions to improper fractions and cancel where possible.

1	$1\frac{3}{4}$	**4**	$3\frac{3}{8}$	**7**	$1\frac{20}{100}$
2	$5\frac{1}{2}$	**5**	$6\frac{7}{10}$	**8**	$2\frac{10}{25}$
3	$2\frac{5}{6}$	**6**	$1\frac{19}{100}$	**9**	$1\frac{400}{1000}$

It is also possible to convert an improper fraction into a mixed fraction – the reverse of the above. For example, $\frac{27}{8}$, $\frac{9}{2}$, $\frac{7}{3}$ and $\frac{11}{10}$ can be converted to mixed fractions. This is done as follows:

Step 1: divide the numerator by the denominator.

Step 2: put the remainder (from the answer in step 1) over the denominator of the improper fraction.

Step 3: combine the whole number (from the answer in step 1) with the answer in step 2.

Example: express the improper fraction $\frac{21}{4}$ as a mixed fraction.

$$5 \text{ remainder } \mathbf{1}$$

Step (1) $4\overline{)21}$

Step (2) $\frac{1}{4}$

Step (3)   combine 5 with $\frac{1}{4}$ to give $5\frac{1}{4}$

So $\frac{21}{4} = 5\frac{1}{4}$

Test 19

Convert the following improper fractions to mixed fractions.

1	$\frac{9}{2}$	**3**	$\frac{16}{3}$	**5**	$\frac{42}{8}$
2	$\frac{23}{4}$	**4**	$\frac{50}{3}$	**6**	$\frac{125}{10}$

Multiplication and division of fractions by whole numbers

Here it is helpful to rewrite the whole number *as an improper fraction with a denominator of 1*, before carrying out the calculation.

For example: 2, 3, 4, 5 etc can be rewritten as

$$\frac{2}{1}, \frac{3}{1}, \frac{4}{1}, \frac{5}{1}$$

Example: $\frac{5}{6} \times 2 = \frac{5}{6} \times \frac{2}{1} = \frac{10}{6} = 1\frac{4}{6} = 1\frac{2}{3}$

Example: $\frac{5}{6} \times 3 = \frac{5}{6} \times \frac{3}{1} = \frac{15}{6} = 2\frac{3}{6} = 2\frac{1}{2}$

Example: $\frac{5}{6} \times 4 = \frac{5}{6} \times \frac{4}{1} = \frac{20}{6} = 3\frac{2}{6} = 3\frac{1}{3}$

Example: $\frac{5}{6} \times 5 = \frac{5}{6} \times \frac{5}{1} = \frac{25}{6} = 4\frac{1}{6}$

Test 20

Multiply or divide the following fractions by the whole numbers shown and express your answers as mixed fractions (questions 1 to 5).

1	$\frac{1}{2} \times 5$	**5**	$\frac{50}{80} \times 12$
2	$\frac{3}{4} \times 6$	**6**	$\frac{3}{4} \div 5$
3	$\frac{7}{8} \times 4$	**7**	$\frac{4}{9} \div 16$
4	$\frac{9}{5} \times 6$	**8**	$\frac{5}{6} \div 20$

How to cross-cancel fractions

Often you can avoid large numbers in nursing calculations by cancelling fractions *diagonally* rather than just top and bottom. Cross-cancelling in this way helps to simplify the arithmetic.

Example: $\frac{7}{8} \times \frac{9}{14}$ without cross-cancelling becomes $\frac{63}{112}$. In cross-cancelling, the 7 can be cancelled diagonally with the 14 (7 goes into 7 once and 7 goes into 14 twice). The calculation then becomes: $\frac{1}{8} \times \frac{9}{2}$ giving $\frac{9}{16}$ as the answer.

Example: $\frac{8}{15} \times \frac{5}{16}$ without cross-cancelling becomes $\frac{40}{240}$. In cross-cancelling, the 8 can be cancelled diagonally with the 16, and the 5 can be cancelled diagonally with the 15. The calculation becomes $\frac{1}{3} \times \frac{1}{2}$ giving $\frac{1}{6}$ as the answer.

It is difficult to cross-cancel 'in your head' so you would normally write the calculation as follows:

$$\frac{\overset{1}{8}}{\underset{3}{15}} \times \frac{\overset{1}{5}}{\underset{2}{16}} = \frac{1}{3} \times \frac{1}{2} = \frac{1}{6}$$

Test 21

Work out the following by cross-cancelling as a first step. Express your answers as mixed fractions or whole numbers.

1 $\frac{7}{3} \times \frac{3}{5}$ **3** $\frac{240}{50} \times \frac{5}{3}$ **5** $\frac{32}{40} \times 80$

2 $\frac{51}{16} \times \frac{4}{3}$ **4** $\frac{3}{10} \times 100$ **6** $\frac{36}{500} \times 1000$

(In the following divisions, cross-cancel after turning the right-hand side number upside down).

7 $\frac{5}{12} \div \frac{16}{24}$ **10** $\frac{40}{150} \div \frac{64}{120}$ **13** $\frac{3}{4} \div \frac{375}{100}$

8 $\frac{17}{100} \div \frac{34}{50}$ **11** $\frac{100}{480} \div \frac{110}{132}$ **14** $\frac{48}{60} \div \frac{80}{360}$

9 $\frac{27}{100} \div \frac{3}{5}$ **12** $\frac{14}{216} \div \frac{28}{36}$ **15** $\frac{15}{100} \div 60$

Test 22

Work out the following by first converting the mixed fractions to improper fractions. The answers are all whole numbers.

1 $4\frac{1}{2} \times \frac{2}{3}$ **4** $20 \div 2\frac{1}{2}$ **7** $5\frac{1}{4} \div 1\frac{3}{4}$

2 $2\frac{4}{5} \times 5$ **5** $1\frac{1}{3} \div \frac{1}{6}$ **8** $\frac{45}{100} \times 2\frac{2}{9}$

3 $4\frac{4}{9} \times 1\frac{4}{5}$ **6** $2\frac{2}{3} \div \frac{8}{15}$ **9** $1\frac{200}{1000} \times 4\frac{1}{6}$

Introduction to decimals

Decimal numbers are numbers that contain a decimal point. *Decimal fractions* are decimal numbers smaller than one (nought point something); they are fractions of a whole number. The decimal point (.) separates the whole number from the fraction.

Decimal in words	Decimal in figures			
	Units	Tenths	Hun.ths	Thou.ths
three point five eight	3.	5	8	
one point two five six	1.	2	5	6
nought point seven three	0.	7	3	

Necessary and unnecessary zeros

It is important to understand which zeros are needed and which are not when writing both whole numbers and decimals. Whole numbers such as 2, 10 and 250 should not be written as 2.0, 10.0 and 250.0 – the decimal point and 0 after it are unnecessary and could lead to errors if misread as 20, 100 and 2500. For a similar reason, a 0 should always be placed in front of the decimal point when there is no other number (example: write 0.73 not .73).

The following are examples of unnecessary zeros:

0.30	0.300	0.3000	which should all be written as 0.3
0.850	0.8500	0.850 00	which should be written as 0.85

The following are examples of necessary zeros:

0.3	0.03	0.003	which all have different values
0.802	0.8002	0.800 02	which all have different values

Test 23

Write out the following numbers in figures

1   twenty two point five
2   nought point two seven five
3   nought point nought two
4   two hundred point zero seven five

Place the numbers (in columns a, b, c and d) in order of size, starting with the *smallest first*. Write a, b, c, d. Take your time and double check.

	(a)	(b)	(c)	(d)
5	2.5	0.25	0.3	0.025
6	0.05	0.1	0.08	0.75
7	3.025	3.25	3.05	3.04
8	6.20	6.02	6.026	6.22
9	10.01	10.101	10.011	10.11

Multiplication by powers of 10 (× 10, × 100, × 1000)

To multiply a decimal number by 10, 100, 1000 etc, you just move the decimal point to the right by however many powers of 10 you have – or put another way, by how many 0s you have (a calculator is not required). To multiply:

   × 10 you move the decimal point one place to the right.
   × 100 you move the decimal point two places to the right.
   × 1000 you move the decimal point three places to the right.

For example: what is 5.178×100?

Answer: $5.178 \times 100 = 517.8$
Similarly: $0.0235 \times 10 = 0.235$

Division by powers of 10 (÷ 10, ÷ 100, ÷ 1000)

Just as in the multiplication of decimals, you can divide decimals by powers of 10 (10, 100, 1000 etc) by moving the decimal point. This is simply the reverse of the multiplication case so when dividing you move the decimal point to the left.

Example:

$$25.34 \quad \div 10 = 2.534$$
$$\div 100 = 0.2534$$
$$\div 1000 = 0.025\,34$$

Other examples are:

$$256.98 \quad \div 100 = 2.5698$$
$$\div 1000 = 0.256\,98$$

Similarly: $0.0037 \div 100 = 0.000\,037$.

Test 24

Work out the following multiplications and divisions. Hint: the number of 0s following the 1 is the number of places to move the decimal point – either to the right (to multiply) or to the left (to divide).

1 $1.5897 \times 1000 =$
2 $7\,692\,105 \div 10\,000 =$
3 $31.729 \times 100 =$
4 $0.175 \div 10 =$
5 $17.1703 \times 1000 =$
6 $0.025 \times 1000 =$
7 $0.0058 \times 1000 =$
8 $0.0001 \times 1\,000\,000 =$

Addition, subtraction, multiplication and division of decimals

The addition and subtraction of decimal numbers is the same as for ordinary numbers. The only thing to remember is to keep the decimal points aligned. Adding unnecessary 0s can help.

Example: $0.36 + 0.28 + 0.052 + 0.1$

$$
\begin{array}{r}
0.360 \\
0.280 \\
0.052 \\
\underline{0.100 \;+} \\
0.792
\end{array}
$$

The multiplication of decimals is similar to the multiplication of whole numbers, with an extra step to work out the position of the decimal point. The 'golden rule' to find the position is:

Number of decimal places (dp) in the question =
Number of dp in answer

Example: 4.21 × 3

4.21	two decimal places
3 ×	no decimal places
12.63	two decimal places in the answer

Example: 0.002 × 0.03

0.002	three decimal places
0.03 ×	two decimal places
0.000 06	five decimal places in the answer

Note that all unnecessary 0s should be removed before you multiply the numbers together.

Test 25

Multiply the following decimal numbers. Treat these as whole numbers first and then add the decimal point as a second step.

1   3.2 × 2.8
2   3.08 × 6.5
3   0.095 × 3.74
4   0.002 × 2.72 (handy hint: place the 0.002 below the 2.72)
5   10.01 × 0.15
6   500 × 0.32 (handy hint: multiply 0.32 by 100 and then by 5)
7   75 × 0.04
8   33.4 × 3
9   800 × 2.54 (handy hint: multiply 2.54 by 100 and then by 8)
10   4000 × 3.50

The division of decimal numbers is carried out in the same way as with whole numbers, leaving the decimal point in the same position.

Example: 24.369 ÷ 3

          8.123   keep the decimal point in
     3⟌24.369   the same position when
                 dividing a decimal number

If the number that you are dividing by contains a decimal point, for example 0.35 or 3.5, then it must be converted to a whole number before the division can take place. To do this you must multiply both numbers by a power of 10 – by 10, 100, 1,000 etc – to remove the decimal point from the number that you are dividing by.

Example: 4.5 ÷ 0.3 becomes 45 ÷ 3 by multiplying both of numbers by 10 to remove the decimal point from the 0.3.

Similarly: 9.375 ÷ 0.02 becomes 937.5 ÷ 2 by multiplying both of the numbers by 100 to remove the decimal point from the 0.02.

These divisions can now be carried out as if they were whole numbers.

Test 26

Work out the following divisions involving decimal numbers. If the number you are *dividing by* contains a decimal point this must be removed first (questions 4 to 11).

1	6.8 ÷ 4	7	3.6 ÷ 0.6
2	62.25 ÷ 5	8	9 ÷ 0.15
3	64.25 ÷ 8	9	1.44 ÷ 1.2
4	6.8 ÷ 0.04	10	125 ÷ 0.002
5	9.99 ÷ 0.3	11	1000 ÷ 0.05
6	5.55 ÷ 0.50	12	0.08 ÷ 5

How to round decimal numbers

Sometimes the numbers you obtain from a calculation are longer than is required for a sensible answer. *Example*: 3.75 × 4.01 =

15.0375. If this level of *accuracy* is not required, you can shorten the number by *rounding it off*. To do this you decrease the number of numbers to the right of the decimal point – that is, you decrease the number of decimal places (dp).

For example, a number such as 15.0375 that has four dp (four numbers to the right of the decimal point) can be rounded off so that it has three, two or one dp.

Method

If the number to the right of the decimal place you are shortening to is 5 or more, then you increase the number in the decimal place by 1; if is less than 5 it remains the same.

Example: round off 15.0375 to three dp – that is, to three numbers to the right of the decimal point.

Answer: The number to the right of the third dp is 5 (15.0375) so we increase the number in the third dp by 1.

15.0375 becomes 15.038.
15.0375 = 15.038 correct to three dp.

Other examples are:

Round off 15.0375 to two dp
Answer: 15.0375 to two dp = 15.04
Round off 15.0375 to one dp
Answer: 15.0375 to one dp = 15.0

Round off 1.976 to 1 decimal place

more than 5 so the
9 becomes a 10 (1 unit)
Answer 1.976 to 1 decimal place = 2.0

Test 27

From the five alternatives choose *one*.

1   6.083 23 to 2 decimal places is:
     6.083   6.08   6.0   6.0832   6.09
2   0.385 426 to 5 decimal places is:
     0.385 43   0.39   0.3854   0.385   0.4
3   0.754 to 1 decimal place is:
     0.75   0.7   0.754   0.8   1.0
4   7.956 to 2 decimal places is:
     7.95   8.0   7.96   7.9   7.956

Test 28

Work out the following and then give your answer to the number of dp shown.

1    $25 \div 6 =$ (to two dp)
2    $100 \div 7 =$ (to four dp)
3    $3.45 \times 3 =$ (to one dp)
4    $14.5 \times 3 =$ (to the nearest whole number = to 0 dp)

Work out the following and then give your answer to the nearest whole number.

5    $325 \div 4 =$ 8 $100 \div 6 =$
6    $1279 \div 8 =$ 9 $73 \div 22 =$
7    $655 \div 10 =$ 10 $400 \div 3 =$

Conversion of decimals to fractions

In order to convert a decimal to a fraction you divide the numbers to the right of the decimal point by:

10 if one number is present
100 if two numbers are present
1000 if three numbers are present etc.

Then cancel the fraction to its lowest terms.

For example: $0.5 = \frac{5}{10} = \frac{1}{2}$
$0.25 = \frac{25}{100} = \frac{1}{4}$
$0.125 = \frac{125}{1000} = \frac{1}{8}$

Test 29

Convert the following decimal numbers to fractions using the method outlined above.

1	0.6	**4**	0.9	**7**	0.95
2	0.75	**5**	0.001	**8**	1.75
3	0.625	**6**	0.08	**9**	2.375

Conversion of fractions to decimals

In nursing and scientific work it is usually more convenient to express a fraction as a decimal. The method is straightforward. All you have to do is divide the denominator (bottom number) into the numerator (top number).

Example: express $\frac{1}{2}$ as a decimal number.

First step: rewrite $\frac{1}{2}$ as $2\overline{)1}$
Second step: rewrite the 1 as 1.0000 by adding a string of zeros.

$$2\overline{)1.0000}$$

This division is carried out in the same way as with ordinary numbers, leaving the decimal point in the same position.
2 into 1 won't go so you put a 0 down and carry the 1 into the next column to make 10. 2 into 10 goes 5 times.

$$\begin{array}{r} 0.5 \\ \hline 2\overline{)1.^{1}0000} \end{array}$$

So $\frac{1}{2}$ expressed as a decimal number is 0.5.

Example: $\frac{5}{8}$ as a decimal $= 8\overline{)5.0000}$

$$\phantom{= 8\overline{)5}}0.6\ 2\ 5$$
$$= 8\overline{)5.^50^20^400}$$
$$= 0.625.$$

Example: $\frac{7}{400}$ as a decimal $= 400\overline{)7.0000}$

$$\phantom{= 400\overline{)7}}0.0\ 1\ 7\ 5$$
$$= 400\overline{)7.^{700}3^{00}0^{200}0}$$
$$= 0.0175$$

Test 30

Express the following fractions as decimal numbers:

1	$\frac{3}{10}$	**4**	$\frac{5}{4}$	**7**	$\frac{17}{20}$
2	$\frac{1}{4}$	**5**	$\frac{3}{25}$	**8**	$\frac{21}{200}$
3	$\frac{2}{5}$	**6**	$\frac{7}{8}$	**9**	$\frac{27}{150}$

How to work out percentages

A percentage (the percentage sign is %) means 'out of 100': in other words something is split into 100 equal parts and each one part is 1 per cent. A percentage is basically a special case of a fraction. *All* percentage fractions have the same bottom number, which is 100. All that changes is the top number.

For example: 3% = (3 ÷ 100)   99% = (99 ÷ 100)

A percentage fraction can be cancelled to its lowest terms:

40% = (40 ÷ 100) which cancels to $\frac{4}{10}$ and finally to $\frac{2}{5}$
12% = (12 ÷ 100) which cancels to $\frac{6}{50}$ and finally to $\frac{3}{25}$

Percentages can also be written in decimal form. To do this we divide the percentage by 100, expressing the answer as a decimal. The easiest way to divide by 100 is to move the decimal point two places to the left.

Example: 40% as a decimal. $40.0 \div 100 = 0.4$

Example: 99% as a decimal. $99.0 \div 100 = 0.99$

Example: 3% as a decimal. $03.0 \div 100 = 0.03$

Test 31

Convert the following percentages to both fractions *and* decimals.

1	20%	4	75%	7	35%
2	25%	5	90%	8	22%
3	10%	6	45%	9	2%

How do you work out the percentage of something? To do this you must multiply the 'something' by the percentage fraction.

Example: find 25% of 60.

First step: $25\% = \frac{25}{100} = \frac{1}{4}$
Second step: $\frac{1}{4} \times 60 = \frac{60}{4} = 15$

Another method is to convert the percentage to a decimal fraction as a first step.

Example: find 25% of 60

First step: $25\% = 25 \div 100 = 0.25$
Second step: $0.25 \times 60 = 15$

In the above example, the fraction method of working out the answer was easier than the decimal method, but in some cases the reverse is true.

Test 32

Work out the following percentages using either the fractions method (questions 1 and 2) or the decimal method (questions 3 and 4).

1   50% of 180
2   30% of 200
3   62.5% of 200
4 $2\frac{1}{2}$% of 1000
5   If 90% of nursing school applicants fail to become nurses what percentage are successful?
6   If there are 90 000 applicants how many will become nurses?

How to express numbers as percentages

We have seen that percentage means out of 100, so:

100% = $\frac{100}{100}$ = 1

This means that we can write any number as a percentage, without affecting its value, by multiplying it by 100% ($\times$ 1).

Whole numbers can be converted to percentages as follows:

Example: 2 × 100% = 200% (2 wholes is 200%)
Similarly: 10 × 100% = 1000% (10 wholes is 1000%)

Fractions can be converted to percentages in the same way:

Example: $\frac{1}{4}$ × 100% = 25%   similarly $\frac{3}{10}$ × 100% = 30%

Decimal fractions can be converted to percentages in the same way, by multiplying by 100%, for example:

0.15 × 100% = 15%   0.01 × 100% = 1%
0.995 × 100% = 99.5%   1.1 × 100% = 110%

Test 33

Convert each decimal or fraction to a percentage by multiplying it by 100%.

1	0.5	**6**	0.015
2	0.75	**7**	1.05
3	1.0	**8**	0.005
4	$\frac{1}{5}$	**9**	$\frac{9}{25}$
5	$\frac{1}{8}$	**10**	$\frac{17}{20}$

Chapter 2 questions

Target = 18 correct answers out of 20 questions.

1 $\frac{1}{5} + \frac{2}{5} =$

2 $\frac{5}{9} - \frac{3}{9} =$

3 $\frac{3}{4} \times \frac{1}{2} =$

4 $\frac{3}{7} \div \frac{3}{2} =$

5 $\frac{5}{32} - \frac{1}{8} =$

6 Cancel $\frac{35}{100}$

7 Convert $\frac{27}{7}$ to a mixed fraction.

8 Convert $4\frac{1}{2}$ to an improper fraction.

9 $\frac{7}{8} \times 7 =$

10 $\frac{3}{10} \div 6 =$

11 Place the following numbers in order of increasing size:
$\frac{3}{4}$, 0.625, 1.2, 0.905, 0.95

12 $1.5 + 0.75 - 0.05 =$

13 Multiply 0.005 by 1000.

14 Multiply 0.8 by 0.9.

15 Divide 62.5 by 1000.

16 Divide 25 by 0.005.

17 Write 8.375 to two dp.

18 Convert $\frac{1}{6}$ to a decimal number; give your answer to 3 dp.

19 Convert 0.0625 to a fraction.

20 What is 5% of 250?

Measurement

The metric system of measurement (SI units)

You will need to familiarize yourself with the metric system of measurements as appropriate to nursing, the most important of which are weight and volume. SI units (international system) are in most cases the same as metric units, all being based on units of 10. The metric system is much easier to understand than the Imperial system (pounds, feet, inches etc).

Weight

The basic unit of weight is the gram (g). All metric weights are based on this. There are four weights you are likely to encounter:

Name	Symbol
kilogram	kg
gram	g
milligram	mg
microgram	mcg or µg

(µ is a Greek symbol pronounced 'mew')

One kilogram is equivalent to 1000 grams.

1 kg = 1000 g and 1 g = $\frac{1}{1000}$ th of a kg.

One gram is equivalent to 1000 mg.

1 g = 1000 mg and 1 mg = $\frac{1}{1000}$ th of a g.

One milligram is equivalent to 1000 mcg.

1 mg = 1000 mcg and 1 mcg = $\frac{1}{1000}$ th of a mg.

We have abbreviated microgram to mcg in preference to µg which can be confused with mg with untidy handwriting when the 'µ' looks like a 'm'. *Confusion can be avoided by writing out the word microgram in full instead of using abbreviations.*

In some calculations it is necessary to convert from one unit of weight to another, for example, grams to milligrams, kilograms to grams.

For example: convert 2 g to milligrams. Since 1 g = 1000 mg, to convert grams to milligrams you multiply by 1000. So 2 g in milligrams is 2 × 1000 = 2000 mg.

Similarly 5.5 kg converted to g is 5.5 × 1000 = 5500 g.

Another example: convert 2200 mg to grams. This time we divide by 1000 because 1 mg = 1/1000th of a gram. So 2200 mg in grams is 2200 ÷ 1000 = 2.2 g.

To convert grams to micrograms you use two steps:

Step 1, convert grams to milligrams.
Step 2, convert milligrams to micrograms.

For example: convert 1.5 g to micrograms.

Step 1: 1.5 g = 1.5 × 1000 mg = 1500 mg.
Step 2: 1500 mg = 1500 × 1000 mcg = 1 500 000 mcg.
So 1.5 g = 1 500 000 micrograms.

From this we can see that one microgram is one thousandth of a milligram and therefore one millionth of a gram, or put another way, there are one million micrograms in one gram.

Choosing the best units for your answer

It is important to choose the most appropriate units for your answer when working with metric quantities. An answer worked out as 1 500 000 micrograms should be written as 1.5 g to avoid a long string of zeros. Similarly an answer of 1500 mg would also be expressed as 1.5 g. However, 0.15 g should be written as 150 mg to avoid the use of a decimal point; similarly 0.15 mg should be expressed as 150 micrograms for the same reason. The following guidelines should be adopted when choosing units.

Guidelines for choosing units of weight

Answers of less than 1 kg (1000 g) are written in grams, for example: 1.5 g, 2.25 g, 20 g, 275 g, 750.5 g, 950 g.

Answers of less than 1 g (1000 mg) are written in milligrams, for example: 1.25 mg, 2.5 mg, 50 mg, 75.1 mg, 450.5 mg.

Answers of less than 1 mg (1000 microgram) are written in micrograms, for example: 2 micrograms, 50 micrograms, 125 micrograms, 750 micrograms.

Answers such as 0.5 mg are non-standard and should be written as 500 micrograms to avoid using a decimal point. However 0.5 can be retained when expressing a range such as 0.5–1 g. The decimal point should always have a leading zero if no whole number is present, so write 0.5 not .5, where the decimal point can easily be missed.

Test 34

Convert the following weights to the metric units specified by moving the decimal point.

1   0.025 mg to micrograms
2   0.001 kg to grams
3   0.33 mg to micrograms
4   1275 mg to grams
5   420 micrograms to mg

Test 35

Express the following metric quantities in the best units (kg, g, mg or micrograms).

1	1000 mg =	**7**	325 µg =
2	2500 mg =	**8**	10 000 mcg =
3	1250 mg =	**9**	1200 g =
4	4500 microgram =	**10**	0.05 g =
5	0.5 g =	**11**	0.5 mg =
6	0.25 g =	**12**	0.000012 g =

Volume

Quantities of liquids are measured in litres (L). You are probably familiar with litres through putting fuel in your car. In nursing you will also meet the millilitre (mL or ml: both can be used but ml is the more common).

A litre is 1000 millilitres:

$1 L = 1000$ ml and 1 ml $= \frac{1}{1000}$ th of 1 ml

Test 36

Convert the following volumes to the metric units specified by moving the decimal point.

1   0.5 L to ml
2   0.05 L to ml
3   1.25 L to ml
4   0.125 L to ml
5   2000 ml to L
6   4050 ml to L
7   5 ml to L
8   250 ml to L
9   10.5 ml to L
10   0.01 L to ml

Test 37

Complete the following review of metric quantities. All of your answers should be *symbols*.

1   kilogram is …
2   litre is …
3   milligram is …
4   microgram is … or …
5   1 gram × 1000 = 1 …
6   1 milligram × 1000 = 1 …
7   1 milligram ÷ 1000 = 1 …
8   1 microgram × 1 000 000 = 1…
9   1 millilitre × 1000 = 1 …

Test 38

Add or subtract the following metric quantities and give your answer in the units shown in the brackets. Hint: the first step is to convert everything to the units stated.

1   1.6 g + 500 mg (in g)
2   1.6 g + 50 mg (in g)
3   2.75 g + 250 mg (in g)
4   1.2 g – 500 mg (in g)
5   0.6 mg + 300 micrograms (in mg)
6   0.01 mg + 425 micrograms (in micrograms)
7   0.5 g + 100 mg + 500 micrograms (in g)
8   750 mcg – 0.075 mg (in micrograms)

Test 39

Multiply or divide the following metric quantities and give your answer in the units specified. Hint: carry out the multiplication first and then convert to the units shown in the brackets afterwards. The 'speed tip' will help you with the multiplication.

1   25 mg × 40 (in g) speed tip: 25 × 40 = 25 × 4 × 10
2   75 mg × 20 (in g) speed tip: 75 × 20 = 75 × 2 × 10
3   50 mcg × 250 (in mg) speed tip: 50 × 250 = 100 × 125
4   125 mcg × 16 (in mg) speed tip: 125 × 16 = 250 × 8 = 500 × 4
5   250 g × 1.2 (in kg) speed tip: 250 × 1.2 = 25 × 12 = 100 × 3

Hint: convert to the units shown in the brackets first and then carry out the division.

6   1 g ÷ 200 (in mg)
7   10 mg ÷ 50 (in micrograms)
8   1.5 mg ÷ 200 (in micrograms)
9   0.004 mg ÷ 8 (in micrograms)
10   1 kg ÷ 400 (in g)

Time

Candidates should be aware that:

60 seconds (sec) = 1 minute (min)
60 minutes = 1 hour (hr, h)
24 hours = 1 day (d)
7 days = 1 week (wk)
52 weeks = 1 year (yr)
am = before noon (midday); pm = afternoon

Candidates should be familiar with both the 12-hour clock (which has two 12-hour periods – am and pm) and the 24-hour clock which starts and finishes at midnight (00:00/24:00 hrs). Noon (midday) = 12:00 hrs (twelve hundred hours). Times can be converted from the 12-hour clock to the 24-hour clock by rewriting the time as a four-digit number and adding 12 hours to all pm times.

Examples: 8.30 am = 08:30 hrs (oh eight thirty hours)
1 pm = 1 + 12 = 13:00 hrs (thirteen hundred hours)
10.45 pm = 10.45 + 12 = 22:45 hrs (twenty two forty five hours)

Likewise, times on the 24-hour clock can be converted to 12-hour clock times by subtracting 12 hours from all afternoon times (those greater than 12:00 hrs).

Example: 20:50 hrs = 20:50 − 12:00 = 8.50 pm

You should be able to convert any fraction of an hour into minutes and any fraction of a minute into seconds.

Examples: $\frac{1}{2}$ hour = 30 minutes
$\frac{1}{4}$ hour = 15 minutes
$\frac{1}{3}$ minute = 20 seconds

Additional examples are:

$\frac{1}{10}$ th hour = $\frac{1}{10} \times \frac{60}{1}$ minutes = 6 minutes
$\frac{3}{5}$ th minute = $\frac{3}{5} \times \frac{60}{1}$ seconds = 3 × 12 = 36 seconds
$2\frac{5}{6}$ th hours = 2 + ($\frac{5}{6} \times \frac{60}{1}$) minutes = 2 hrs 50 minutes
0.75 hours = 0.75 × 60 minutes = 45 minutes
0.2 hours = 0.2 × 60 minutes = 12 minutes
2.4 hours = 2 + (0.4 × 60) minutes = 2 hrs 24 minutes

Test 40

Work out following clock times and complete the calculations involving measurements of time.

1   Write 6.25 am as a 24-hour clock time
2   Write 5.05 pm as a 24-hour clock time
3   Write 21:50 hrs as a 12-hour clock time
4   Write 10:10 hrs as a 12-hour clock time
5   What time is it when 1.5 hours is added to 6 pm?
6   What time is it when 3.25 hours is added to 22:30 hours?
7   Write 93 minutes in hours and minutes
8   Convert 0.3 hours to minutes
9   Convert 2.2 minutes to seconds
10   Express 40 seconds as a fraction of 1 minute
11   How many seconds are there in 0.9 minutes?
12   How many seconds are there in 0.33 minutes? (give your answer to the nearest second)

Reading instrument scales

A scale is a set of marks on a line used for measuring. Examples are found on rulers, measuring jugs, blood pressure gauges and patients' observation charts. Scales usually have regular spaces (intervals) between the 'tick marks' (*graduation* lines), for example, millimetres on rulers. Most scales begin at zero with the graduation lines spread evenly along the length. Other scales are circular with the graduation spread evenly around a dial, as seen on a blood pressure gauge.

The key to reading any scale is in knowing how many intervals there are between the numbers. The metric system is based on units of 10, and metric scales normally have 10 intervals. A 15 cm (6 inch) ruler, for example, has each centimetre divided into 10 millimetres. Here are some examples of graduated scales.

Measuring jug: 750 ml full (halfway between 700 and 800 ml):

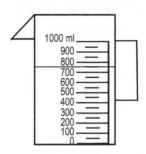

Measuring jug: 50 ml full (halfway between 0 and 100 ml):

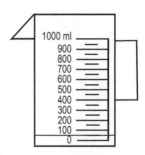

Graduated syringes (not drawn to scale):

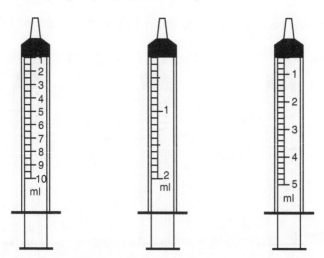

On the 10 ml syringe on the left there are two graduations for every 1 ml, so each graduation mark represents 0.5 ml (each ml is divided into two equal parts).

On the 2 ml syringe in the middle there are 10 graduations for every 1 ml, so each graduation mark represent 0.1 ml (each ml is divided into 10 equal parts).

On the 5 ml syringe on the right there are five graduations for every 1 ml, so each graduation mark represent 0.2 ml (each ml is divided into five equal parts).

Use the above information to work out the volume of solution in each of the 12 syringes shown on the following pages. Some of the syringes are of 1 ml capacity, and as a first step you will need to work out the volume represented by one graduation mark using the method outlined above.

Test 41

What is the volume in millilitres shown by the horizontal line?

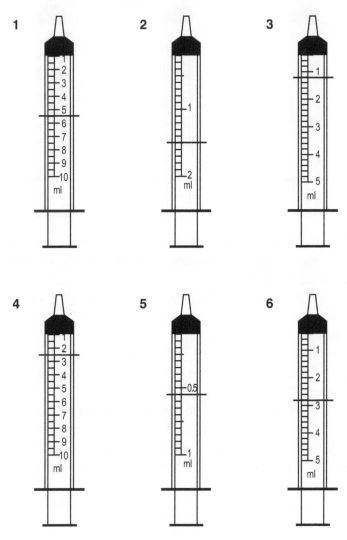

Test 42

What is the volume in millilitres shown by the horizontal line?

1
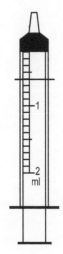

2
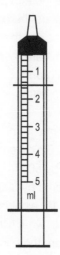

3

4
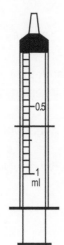

5
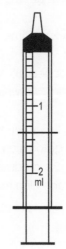

6
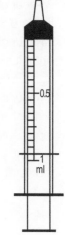

Chapter 3 questions

1   How many grams are there in 2000 milligrams?
2   How many milligrams are there in 0.4 g?
3   How many micrograms are there in 0.25 mg?
4   How many micrograms are there in 0.01 mg?
5   Convert 0.08 g to milligrams.
6   Convert 0.0075 L to millilitres.
7   What is 5 g + 500 mg?
8   Express 950 micrograms in milligrams.
9   Add 7 g + 654 mg + 320 micrograms?
10 What is 10 g divided by 500?
11 Multiply 500 micrograms by 300.
12 If 100 ml is added to 1L, what is the new volume in litres?
13 If 25 ml is added to 1L, what is the new volume in litres?
14 How many millilitres are there in 0.062 L?
15 How many millilitres are there in 0.5775 L?
16 If it is 5.30 pm now, what time will it be in six hours on the 24-hour clock?
17 If it is 8.30 pm now, what time will it be in 12 hours on the 24-hour clock?
18 An infusion was stopped at 10.15 am and then started again three hours later. At what time did it restart, on the 24-hour clock?
19 A 1 ml syringe has 20 graduation marks. What volume is represented by each graduation mark?
20 A 5 ml syringe has 25 graduation marks. What volume is represented by 20 graduation marks?

Drug dosage calculations

Oral medications

The easiest drug calculations to perform are those that involve oral medications. These medications are usually dispensed as tablets or capsules, or sometimes as liquids if the patient has difficulty swallowing.

Calculations for tablets involve wholes. For example, 1 gram of paracetamol requires two 500 milligram tablets; only scored tablets may be split in half. Most liquid medications (syrups, elixirs, suspensions, mixtures, linctuses and emulsions) are measured out in millilitres, often in multiples of the 5 ml spoon. For example, 'take two 5 ml spoonfuls three times daily'. If the dose is less than 5 ml it is measured out with an oral syringe.

There is a general equation that applies to all oral medications:

Number of Measures administered equals Dosage Prescribed divided by Dosage per Measure

No of measures = dose prescribed ÷ dose per measure

Expressed mathematically as an equation this is:

$$\textbf{Number of measures} = \frac{\text{Dose prescribed}}{\text{Dose per measure}}$$

In oral medications the 'measure' is most frequently a tablet, a capsule or a spoonful.

Example: a doctor prescribes a dose of 15 mg of a drug. This drug is supplied in 5 mg tablets. How many tablets are given?

The 'measure' in this case is a tablet, so the equation can be rewritten as:

$$\textbf{Number of tablets} = \frac{\text{Dose prescribed}}{\text{Dose per tablet}}$$

$$= \frac{15\text{ mg}}{5\text{ mg}} = 3\text{ tablets}$$

Key point: You must make sure that the units are the same for both the prescribed dosage and dosage per tablet.

Example: 1.2 grams of a drug is prescribed. Each tablet contains 600 mg of the drug. How many tablets are to be dispensed?

Note that the units are not the same (grams and milligrams) so we need to convert one unit into the other unit as a first step. In most cases it is easiest to convert the bigger unit into the smaller unit, so convert grams into milligrams. We do this by multiplying by 1000.

First step: 1.2 g = 1.2 × 1000 = 1200 mg (see the metric system).
Second step:

$$\textbf{Number of tablets} = \frac{\text{Dose prescribed}}{\text{Dose per tablet}}$$

$$= \frac{1200\text{ mg}}{600\text{ mg}} = 2\text{ tablets}$$

As a rough 'rule of thumb' a reasonable number of tablets is 0.5 to 4. So if your calculation shows that the patient needs 10 tablets you have probably made a mistake.

Note: a patient on high dose steroids may take as many as 12 5 mg tablets of prednisolone in a single dose; this is the exception that proves the rule of thumb.

Example: a syrup is prescribed. The syrup has 4 mg of drug per 5 ml spoonful. If the patient needs 12 mg, how many spoonfuls are needed?

The measure in this case is a spoonful so the equation can be rewritten as:

$$\textbf{Number of spoonfuls} = \frac{\text{Dose prescribed}}{\text{Dose per spoonful}}$$

$$= \frac{12\ \text{mg}}{4\ \text{mg}} = 3\ \text{spoonfuls}$$

Key point: If the question asks for the volume of drug needed, the size of the spoonful (the measure) needs to be taken into account and a further step is required. We have three spoonfuls of 5 ml each:

3 spoonfuls = 3 'lots' of 5 ml = 3 × 5 ml = 15 ml

Example: a patient needs 50 mg of a drug. The stock bottle contains 25 mg per 5 ml spoonful. How many ml should be measured out?

$$\textbf{Number of ml} = \frac{\text{Dose prescribed}}{\text{Dose per measure}}\ \textbf{'lots of 5 ml'}$$

$$= \frac{50\ \text{mg}}{25\ \text{mg}} \times 5\ \text{ml}$$

$$= 2 \times 5\ \text{ml} = 10\ \text{ml}$$

Example: a patient needs 300 mg of a drug. If the stock bottle contains 100 mg in 10 ml, how many ml should be drawn up?

$$\textbf{Number of ml} = \frac{\text{Dose prescribed}}{\text{Dose per measure}} \text{ 'lots of 10 ml'}$$

$$= \frac{300 \text{ mg}}{100 \text{ mg}} \times 10 \text{ ml} = 3 \times 10 \text{ ml} = 30 \text{ ml}$$

You can check your answer as follows: 30 ml = 3 lots of 10 ml; 3 lots of 100 mg = 300 mg (correct dose).

Test 43

No of Measures = Dose Prescribed ÷ Dose per Measure

1   A drug in tablet form is prescribed. The required dosage is 75 mg. The tablets are in 25 mg each. How many tablets should be dispensed?

2   The patient is written up for 500 micrograms of a drug and each tablet contains 0.25 mg. How many tablets are required?

3   30 mg of a drug is prescribed. The drug is in liquid form and is to be given orally. It has strength of l0 mg per 5 ml spoon.
   a) How many spoonfuls are required?
   b) What volume is dispensed?

4   60 mg of a drug is prescribed. The drug is in liquid form and is to be given orally. It has strength of 30 mg per 5 ml spoon.
   a) How many spoonfuls are required?
   b) What volume is dispensed?

5   A patient requires 20 mg of a drug in liquid form. If the stock contains 10 mg in 2 ml, what volume of the drug should be drawn up?

6   1.5 milligrams of a drug are prescribed. Each tablet contains 500 micrograms. How many tablets should be dispensed?

7   A patient requires 500 micrograms of a drug and each tablet contains 0.125 mg. How many tablets are required?

8 A patient requires 200 micrograms of a drug orally. The stock contains 0.1 mg in 5 ml. How many 5 ml spoonfuls should be administered?

9 The bottle contains 100 milligrams of a drug per 5 ml. What dose will the patient receive if 20 ml is measured out?

10 The stock contains 250 micrograms per 2 ml. What dose will the patient receive if 10 ml is measured out?

Injections

Drugs for injection are normally supplied in ampoules or vials. Glass ampoules have to be broken off at the neck (a dot marks the weak spot). The ampoule is inverted and the solution is withdrawn with a needle and syringe. Glass vials, with rubber stoppers, are used to contain drugs in powdered form. The drug has to be reconstituted with a diluent, typically sterilized water, before use.

A needle and syringe are used to add the water to a vial and the mixture is shaken to reconstitute the drug. The reconstituted drug is then drawn up into the syringe. Some powdered drugs displace water, in which case the volume of water to add is always less than the final volume in the vial. For example: to make 10 ml of solution add 9.8 ml of sterilized water. Here the *displacement volume* is 0.2 ml.

Calculating drug dosages for injection is very similar to calculating oral doses. However, the dose prescribed is often less than the dose per measure, so you must be able to cancel fractions to their lowest terms and also be able to convert fractions to decimals.

Example: a vial contains 1 mg of a drug in 10 ml of solution. How many millilitres need to be drawn up for a dose of:

a)   500 micrograms?   b)   50 micrograms?
c)   250 micrograms?   d)   1500 micrograms?

The first step is to convert the 1 mg dose to micrograms:

$\quad$ 1 mg = 1 × 1000 micrograms = 1000 micrograms

The second step uses the equation:

$$\textbf{Number of ml} = \frac{\text{Dose prescribed}}{\text{Dose per measure}} \times 10 \text{ ml}$$

a) Number of ml = $\frac{500}{1000}$ × 10 ml = $\frac{1}{2}$ × $\frac{10}{1}$ = $\frac{10}{2}$ = 5 ml

(Method: cancel the fraction to its lowest terms, multiply it by 10 and convert the improper fraction to a whole number.)

b) Number of ml = $\frac{50}{1000}$ × 10 ml = $\frac{1}{20}$ × $\frac{10}{1}$ = $\frac{10}{20}$ = $\frac{1}{2}$ = 0.5 ml

(Method: cancel the fraction to its lowest terms, multiply it by 10, cancel the fraction to its lowest terms and convert it to a decimal number.)

c) Number of ml = $\frac{250}{1000}$ × 10 ml = $\frac{1}{4}$ × $\frac{10}{1}$ = $\frac{10}{4}$ = $\frac{5}{2}$ = 2.5 ml

(Method: same as in b.)

d) Number of ml = $\frac{1500}{1000}$ × 10 ml = $\frac{3}{2}$ × $\frac{10}{1}$ = $\frac{30}{2}$ = 15 ml

(Method: cancel the improper fraction to its lowest terms, multiply it by 10 and cancel the improper fraction to its lowest terms.)

Test 44

ml = dose prescribed ÷ dose per measure × volume of measure (a, b, c or d).

1   An oral solution contains 100 mg of drug in every 5 ml. How many ml must be drawn up for a dose of:

   a) 10 mg?   b) 15 mg?   c) 20 mg?   d) 30 mg?

2   A vial contains 1 mg of a drug in every 4 ml of solution. How many ml need to be drawn up for a dose of:

   a) 750 mcg?   b) 500 mcg?   c) 250 mcg?   d) 100 mcg?

3   A solution contains 2.5 mg of a drug per 10 ml. How many ml need to be drawn up for a dose of:

   a) 1.25 mg?   b) 500 mcg?   c) 625 mcg?   d) 250 mcg?

4   A bottle of medication contains 1 mg per 10 ml. How many ml are drawn into the syringe for a dose of:

   a) 2 mg?   b) 1.5 mg?   c) 0.1 mg?   d) 500 mcg?

Infusions, the giving set and drop rates

In this section a further factor is introduced into drug dosage calculations, that of *time*. Some fluids have to be *infused* into the body slowly over several hours. The treatment sheet will indicate the amount of time required for the prescribed dose: for example, 1 litre over 8 hours. In some infusions a 'giving set' can be used to control the speed of the infusion; a drip chamber allows the nurse to see the drops and to set the drop rate. The drop rate is dependent on the volume to be infused, the time of the infusion and the size of each drop.

   Key point: in a standard giving set the volume of each drop is of one-twentieth of a millilitre or 0.05 ml. This means that there are 20 drops in every 1 ml; there are 20 drops per millilitre.

The speed of the drops, or drop rate, needs to be calculated in drops per minute. Calculations involving drop rates usually require conversion from ml per hour to drops per minute.

Example: 250 ml of fluid is to be given over two hours using a standard giving set (20 drops per ml). What is the drop rate?
Step 1: convert to ml/hr.
Step 2: convert to drops/hr.
Step 3: convert to drops/minute.

Step 1: 250 ml in 2 hours = 250 ÷ 2 = 125 ml/hr.
Step 2: 125 × 20 = 2500 drops/hr.
Step 3: 2500 ÷ 60 cancels to 250 ÷ 6 then cancels to 125 ÷ 3.

$$\frac{41.67}{3 \overline{\smash{)}125.00}} = 42 \text{ drops per minute (to the nearest drop)}$$

Example: 1.5 litres is to be given over six hours using a standard giving set. What is the correct drop rate for the infusion?

Step 1: 1.5 litres in 6 hours = 1500 ÷ 6 = 250 ml/hr.
Step 2: 250 × 20 = 5000 drops/hr.
Step 3: 5000 ÷ 60 = $\frac{5000}{60}$ = $\frac{500}{6}$ = $\frac{250}{3}$ = 83 drops/minute (to the nearest drop).

Test 45

A standard giving set delivers 1 ml for every 20 drops.

1   Convert the following infusion rates to drops per minute. The giving set has 20 drops per ml.

a) 200 ml in 40 minutes   b) 120 ml in 30 minutes
c) 80 ml in 100 minutes   d) 90 ml in 1 hour

2   Convert the following infusion rates to drops per minute. The giving set has 20 drops per ml. Give your answers to the nearest drop.

a) 200 ml/hr   b) 250 ml/hr
c) 500 ml in 6 hrs   d) 1 L in 8 hrs

Concentration

The term *concentration* means the strength of the solution that contains the drug. By way of example, instant coffee is made by dissolving coffee power in hot water; you can make the drink (the *solution*) either strong or weak depending on the volume of water (the *diluent*) added and the quantity of coffee used. Two spoonfuls of coffee in 200 ml of water gives the same strength drink as one spoonful in 100 ml of water. Similarly, a vial containing 2 mg of a drug in 20 ml of solution is the same strength as vial containing 1 mg of the same drug in 10 ml of solution. Different strengths are easily compared by considering how much drug is present in each 1 ml of solution (per ml; /ml).

Example: a vial contains 2.5 mg of a drug in 5 ml of solution. What is the concentration of the drug in mg per ml?

2.5 mg of drug are contained in 5 ml of solution so 1 ml must contain only one-fifth as much drug.
2.5 mg is contained in 5 ml so 1 ml contains 2.5 ÷ 5 = 0.5 mg per ml or 0.5 mg/ml.

The concentration is 0.5 mg/ml (0.5 mg of drug in every 1 ml).
Concentrations can also be used to work out the quantity of drug in a given volume of solution.

Example: the concentration of a drug is 0.5 mg/ml. How many milligrams of drug are there in 1 litre?

First step: 1 litre = 1000 ml.
Second step: 0.5 mg in 1 ml and we have 1000 ml.
So milligrams of drug = 0.5 × 1000 = 500 mg.

Example: the concentration of a drug is 250 milligram/ml. How many grams are there in 100 ml?

First step: 250 mg = 250 ÷ 1000 g = 0.25 g.
Second step: 0.25 g in 1 ml and we have 100 ml.
So grams of drug = 0.25 × 100 = 25 g (25 g/100 ml).

*Key point: the concentration of infusion fluids is usually measured in terms of **percentage weight-volume (% w/v)**, where the weight (w) is in **grams** and the volume (v) is **100 ml**.*

So 1% w/v means 1 g per 100 ml of solution, 2% w/v means 2 g per 100 ml of solution etc.

'Sodium chloride 0.9% w/v infusion fluid' has 0.9 g of sodium chloride dissolved in 100 ml of water.

Example: a 1 litre bag of saline (sodium chloride solution) is labelled as 0.9% w/v. How many grams of sodium chloride are there in the bag?

First step: 0.9% w/v **means** 0.9 g per 100 ml (0.9 g/100 ml).
Second step: 1 litre = 1000 ml = 10 × 100 ml.
$$= 10 \times 0.9\,g = 9\,g.$$

Example: a 5 ml vial contains a drug at a strength of 0.1% w/v. How many milligrams are there in 1 ml of solution?

First step: 0.1% w/v means 0.1 g/100 ml.
Second step: convert 0.1 g to mg.
$$0.1\,g = 0.1 \times 1000\,mg = 100\,mg$$
So we have 100 mg/100 ml or 1 mg/1 ml (1 mg/ml).

From the above answer we can see that:

1 mg/ml = 0.1% w/v; 2 mg/ml = 0.2% w/v;
10 mg/ml = 1% w/v; 50 mg/ml = 5% w/v etc.

Bags of saline labelled as 0.9% w/v contain sodium chloride at a concentration of 9 mg/ml, which is similar to that of blood plasma, making it safe to infuse in large quantities. It is known as *physiological saline* ('normal saline').

If you come across *percentage weight-weight (% w/w)*, it means that both the drug and the diluent are measured by weight. In this case 1% w/w means 1 g per 100 g.

Test 46

Complete the following concentration questions. They do not require any knowledge of drugs.

1   You have lidocaine (lignocaine) for injection, 40 mg in 2 ml ampoules. What is the concentration in mg/ml?
2   You have lidocaine (lignocaine) for injection, 100 mg in 10 ml ampoules. What is the concentration in mg/ml?
3   A syringe contains 20 mg of morphine in 8 ml. What is the concentration of morphine in mg/ml?
4   500 mg of amoxicillin powder is dissolved in 12.5 ml of water. What is the concentration in mg/ml?
5   1 g of amoxicillin powder is dissolved in 20 ml of water. What is the concentration in mg/ml?
6   How many grams of glucose are there in a 500 ml bag of 5% w/v glucose infusion fluid?
7   The patient is to receive an intravenous infusion of sodium chloride (0.18% w/v) and glucose (4% w/v). How much glucose is present in a 500 ml bag?
8   Zinc and castor oil ointment contains 7.5% w/w zinc oxide. How much zinc oxide is present in a 25 g tube of ointment?
9   Danaparoid sodium (Orgaran®) contains 1250 units/ml. How many units are there in a 0.6 ml ampoule?
10 10 ml of sterile water is added to a vial containing 500 mg of clarithromycin (Klaricid®). What is a) the concentration of the reconstituted drug in mg/ml? and b) the approximate concentration of the infusion fluid in mg/ml if the 10 ml of solution is added to a 250 ml bag of 5% glucose?

Higher-level calculations

These are longer questions that require additional steps to arrive at the answer. The key to answering these questions is to break them down into manageable chunks. This is done by making the more obvious calculations first, often starting with the information contained in the first sentence.

In the example below, the dose required is *proportional* to the patient's weight. So, for example, a patient weighing 100 kg will require twice the dose of a patient weighing 50 kg.

The *dose* is given in milligrams per kilogram (of body weight) per hour, (mg/kg/hr).

The *infusion rate* is given in millilitres per hour (ml/hr).

The *drop rate* is given in drops per minute (drops/min).

Example: the treatment sheet indicates that you need to administer 1 g of a drug at a rate of 10 mg/kg/hr. The bag contains 1 g in 100 ml. If the patient weighs 80 kg, then:

a) what is the drop rate for a standard giving set?

b) how long should the infusion last?

The question looks complicated but is easily broken down into manageable chunks as follows:

a) Step 1:   The patient needs 10 mg per kg per hour
            $= 10 \times 80$ mg per hour
            $= 800$ mg/hr (the dose prescribed per hour).

    Step 2:   Work out the volume of drug required per hour.
            No of ml $=$ Dose prescribed $\div$ Dose per bag $\times$ Volume of vial
            $= (800 \div 200) \times$ Volume of vial
            $= 0.8 \times 100$
            $= 80$ ml/hr.

    Step 3:   Work out the number of drops for a standard giving set.
            80 ml $\times$ 20 drops $= 1600$ drops per hour

    Step 4:   Work out the drop rate in drops per minute.
            $= 1600 \div 60$
            $= 80 \div 3$
            $= 27$ drops/minute to the nearest drop.

b) To work out the length of the infusion we return to Step 2. The rate of the infusion is 800 mg/hr and we have to administer 1 g (1000 mg). The time of the infusion is given by:
    $\frac{1000}{800}$ hrs $= \frac{10}{8} = \frac{5}{4} = 1\frac{1}{4}$ hours

(Check: 800 mg/hr $\times$ 1.25 hr $= 1000$ mg.)

Test 47

1 The treatment is a continuous intravenous infusion of dopamine. You have 400 mg of the drug, ready-mixed in 250 ml of 5% glucose infusion fluid. The rate of the infusion is to be 3 microgram/kg/minute and the patient weighs 89 kg. Calculate:

a) the concentration of dopamine in the infusion fluid, in mg/ml

b) the rate in micrograms/minute

c) the rate in milligrams/minute

d) the rate in milligrams/hour (to 1 decimal place)

e) the rate in ml/hour (refer to your answer in a).

2 The prescription requires 40 microgram/kg/hr of diclofenac sodium (Voltarol®) to be given by an intravenous infusion. The stock is a 3 ml 25 mg/ml ampoule to be diluted to 500 ml with infusion fluid. If the patient weighs 75 kg calculate:

a) the number of milligrams of Voltarol® in one 500 ml bag

b) the rate in micrograms/hour

c) the rate in mg/hour

d) the concentration of Voltarol® in the infusion fluid in mg/ml

e) the infusion rate in ml/hour

f) how many hours the infusion fluid will last.

3 The patient is written up for gentamicin 80 mg to be infused over 30 minutes in a 100 ml bag of 0.9% w/v sodium chloride. You have 1 ml ampoules containing 40 mg/ml. If the drug is gravity fed using a 20 drop/ml giving set, calculate:

a) the total volume of the infusion fluid (after adding the drug to the bag)

b) the infusion rate in drops per minute.

4 Lidocaine (lignocaine) is to be given by intravenous infusion at a rate of 4 mg/minute. Stock is 0.2% w/v lidocaine in 5% w/v glucose infusion fluid. What is the infusion rate in ml/hour?

5   A patient weighing 100 kg is to receive an intravenous infusion of amiodarone 5 mg/kg over 2 hours. Stock is 3 ml ampoules containing 50 mg/ml and the diluent is 250 ml of 5% w/v glucose. Calculate:

a) the number of milligrams of amiodarone to be administered
b) the volume of amiodarone to be drawn up in millilitres
c) the number of whole ampoules required to do this (round up)
d) the total volume of fluid to be infused
e) the rate of infusion rate in ml/hour.

6   A patient weighing 100 kg requires an intravenous infusion of sodium nitroprusside 1.5 micrograms/kg/minute given in 1 L of 5% glucose solution for 3 hours. The stock is a 10 mg/ml 5 ml vial. Calculate:

a) the number of milligrams of drug to infuse
b) the volume of drug to be drawn up from the 5 ml vial.

7   The treatment is N-acetylcysteine (Parvolex®) 50 mg/kg diluted in 500 ml of 5% glucose, for infusion over 4 hours. The drug comes in 10 ml ampoules of concentration 200 mg/ml. For a patient weighing 85 kg, calculate:

a) the number of grams of Parvolex® to infuse
b) the exact number of ampoules required
c) the total volume of solution to infuse
d) the infusion rate in ml/minute to one decimal place.

8   You are to administer a continuous intravenous infusion of dobutamine 5 microgram/kg/minute to a patient weighing 83 kg. Stock is a 20 ml ampoule containing 125 mg of dobutamine per ml. The entire contents are diluted with sodium chloride 0.9% w/v infusion fluid. How long will the solution last, to the nearest hour?

Changing the infusion rate

Some questions will ask you to work out a new infusion time or a new infusion rate, where the speed of an infusion is altered part-way through. The key is to break the question into two parts. First, you have to work out the volume given before the infusion was stopped; and then the volume left to give when the infusion is restarted (and the time left to give it where the new rate is to be calculated).

Example: a 2 L bag of 0.9% saline is infused at a rate of 125 ml/hr for the first 6 hours and then increased to 150 ml/hr until the bag is finished. How long will the infusion last?

1) 125 ml/hr for 6 hours = 6 × 125 = 750 ml
2) Remainder = 2000 ml – 750 ml = 1250 ml
1250 ml ÷ 150 ml/hr = $\frac{1250}{150} = \frac{125}{15} = \frac{25}{3} = 8\frac{1}{3}$ = 8 hr 20 min
Total time = 6 hr + 8 hr 20 min = 14 hr 20 min

Example: a 2 L bag of 0.9% saline is infused at a rate of 150 ml/hr for the first 8 hours. The rate is then decreased so that the infusion is complete after a further 8 hours. Calculate the new infusion rate in ml/hr.
1) 150 ml/hr for 8 hours = 8 × 150 = 1200 ml
2) Remainder = 2000 – 1200 ml = 800 ml
800 ml ÷ 8 hr = 100 ml/hr

Test 48

1   An infusion of 1 litre of 0.9% saline is required. The pump is switched on at 08:30 hours and the flow rate is 100 ml/hour. After 4 hours the pump speed is reduced to 60 ml/hr. At what time will the infusion be complete?

2   A 1.5 L litre bottle of Jevity® liquid is PEG tube fed via a pump. The rate is set to 125 ml/hr and the pump is switched on at 20:00 hours. The rate is increased at 06:00 hours. If the feed has finished by 07:00 hours, what was the rate increased to?

Calculating the prescribed dose in infusions

If you know the concentration of the drug and the speed of the pump it is possible to work 'backwards' to find the prescribed dose in, for example, mg/minute or microgram/kg/minute.

Example: a pump containing 250 mg of furosemide in 50 ml of solution is running at 48 ml/hr. What is the dose in mg/minute?

Step 1: The concentration in mg/ml: 250 mg ÷ 50 ml = 5 mg/ml.
Step 2: Convert the speed from ml/hr to ml/min:
    48 ml/hr ÷ 60 min/hr = ml/min = 0.8 ml/min.
Take one minute: volume = 0.8 ml (step 2) and then the dose is:
    0.8 ml × 5 mg/ml (in step 1) = 4 mg in one minute or 4 mg/min.

Example: a syringe pump contains 25 mg of dobutamine in 50 ml of solution. The pump is running at a speed of 72 ml/hr. What is the dose in micrograms/kg/minute for an 80 kg patient?

Step 1: Work out the concentration in micrograms/ml:
    25 mg ÷ 50 ml = 0.5 mg/ml = 500 micrograms/ml.
Step 2: Work out the concentration in micrograms/kg/ml.
    500 micrograms/ml ÷ 80 kg = 50 ÷ 8 = 6.25 micrograms/kg/ml.
Step 3: Convert the speed from ml/hr to ml/min:
    72 ml/hr ÷ 60 min/hr = $\frac{6}{5}$ = 1.2 ml/min.
    Take one minute: volume = 1.2 ml (step 3) and the dose is then:
6.25 microgram/kg × 1.2 ml (in step 2) = 7.5 microgram/kg in one minute or 7.5 microgram/kg/min.

Test 49

1   Calculate the dose of dobutamine in microgram/kg/minute for the following pump rates and patient body weights. The concentration of dobutamine in the syringe is 500 microgram/ml.
    a) pump rate: 7.2 ml/hr; body weight: 60 kg
    b) pump rate: 5.4 ml/hr; body weight: 90 kg
    c) pump rate: 30 ml/hr; body weight: 100 kg
    d) pump rate: 75 ml/hr body weight: 50 kg.

Chapter 4 questions

1   The prescription asks for bumetanide 4 mg. Stock is 1 mg tablets. How many do you give?

2   A vial contains furosemide (frusemide) 10 mg/ml. How much do you draw up for a dose of 20 mg?

3   The patient is prescribed 30 mg of metoclopramide by sub-cutaneous infusion. Stock is 5 mg/ml in 2 ml vials. How many vials are required?

4   The patient has been prescribed ranitidine (Zantac®) 150 mg. Stock is Zantac syrup, 75 mg/5 ml. How much do you give?

5   What volume of amitriptyline 25 mg/5 ml oral solution is required to give a dose of 75 mg?

6   You are to administer 5 mg of oral morphine (Oramorph®). Stock vials contain 10 mg/5 ml. How much do you give?

7   Erythromycin is prescribed. 1 g of powder is reconstituted with 'water for injection' to give 20 ml of solution. What volume of the solution should be added to the infusion bag for a dose of 900 mg?

8   100 ml of reconstituted ciprofloxacin suspension contains 5 g of the drug. How much do you give if the treatment sheet asks for 750 mg?

9   The patient needs 120 mg of procainamide by intravenous injection. If it is given at a rate of 30 mg/minute how long will the injection take?

10 If an infusion pump delivers 40 ml in 30 minutes, what is the infusion rate in ml/hour?

11 30 mg of midazolam (Hypnovel®) is to be infused over 12 hours. What is the infusion rate in mg/hour?

12 Quinine 20 mg/kg is infused over 4 hours. What is the dose per hour for a patient weighing 74 kg?

13 Ketamine is to be given by intramuscular injection. The dose is 10 mg/kg and the stock is a 100 mg/ml 10 ml vial. How much do you draw up for a patient weighing 82 kg?

14 Your patient has been written up for an intravenous infusion of terbutaline. A 500 micrograms/ml 5 ml ampoule is diluted with

glucose 5% to a concentration of 10 micrograms/ml for infusion over 10 hours. What is the infusion rate in ml/hour?

15   Zovirax® cream (aciclovir 5% w/w) is prescribed. How much aciclovir is present in a 2 g tube of cream?

16   One litre of physiological saline (0.9% w/v) is to be given over 6 hours with a 20 drop per ml giving set. What is the drop rate in drops per minute (to the nearest drop)?

17   1 g of amoxicillin is reconstituted with 'water for injection' to give 20 ml of solution. What is the concentration of the drug in mg/ml?

18   500 mg of amoxicillin powder is reconstituted with 2.5 ml of 'water for injection' and then diluted to 50 ml with 0.9% sodium chloride infusion fluid. What is the concentration of the drug in mg/ml?

19   A 2.5 g dose of flucytosine is administered over 30 minutes by intravenous infusion. Stock is a 10 mg/ml infusion bottle. What is the volume infused?

20   A syringe pump containing 250 mg of furosemide in 125 ml of solution is running at a speed of 90 ml/hr. What is the dose in mg/minute?

CHAPTER 5

Drug administration

Equation-free drug calculations

While basic drug dosage calculations can be carried out with a simple equation (eg dose prescribed/dose per measure), more difficult questions can be harder to conceptualize. That is to say, it can be difficult to decide what numbers go where and what steps are needed to arrive at the correct answer.

Fortunately there is an alternative method for solving more complex problems (which also works with simple calculations). This section will explain how to calculate drug dosages without referring to an equation. If you can get to grips with this method (and it is not difficult) you do not need to remember any equations, nor do you need any real understanding of the mathematical steps!

Drug calculations that use equations focus on the numbers, with the units added in at the end. In an equation-free method, the units are placed at the centre of the calculation with the numbers left until the end. The process is known as a 'dimensional analysis' and it requires little mathematical knowledge.

There are three basic units or dimensions, which are length (used for lengths, areas and volumes), weight (or mass), and time.

In nursing calculations, these dimensions are represented by the metric units litre (L), millilitre (ml), kilogram (kg), milligram (mg), microgram and time (sec, min and hrs).

In equation-free calculations the units are used to guide the arithmetic process. The method involves cancelling (eliminating) the units that we do not want, leaving behind the units required for the answer. It is worth reviewing how units can be multiplied and divided before we begin drug dosage calculations with this new method.

The following examples show how units and numbers can be worked out separately from each other. It is vital that you understand the examples written beneath the heading 'Weight'.

Length:

i) 10×5 cm $= (10 \times 5)$ cm $= 50$ cm

ii)   10 cm $\times$ 5 cm $= (10 \times 5)$ cm $\times$ cm $= 50$ cm^2 (50 cm squared)

iii)   10 cm $\times$ 5 cm $\times$ 3 cm $= 150$ cm $\times$ cm $\times$ cm $= 150$ cm^3 (150 cm cubed)

iv)   10 cm $\div$ 5 $= (10 \div 5)$ cm $= 2$ cm

v)   10 cm^3 $\div$ 5 cm $= (10 \div 5)$ cm^3 $\div$ cm $= 2$ cm^2

vi)   10 cm^2 $\div$ 5 cm $= (10 \div 5)$ cm^2 $\div$ cm $= 2$ cm

vii)   10 cm $\div$ 5 cm $= (10 \div 5)$ cm $\div$ cm $= 2$ (no units)

Weight:

viii) 10×5 mg $= (10 \times 5)$ mg $= 50$ mg

ix)   10 mg $\times$ 5 mg $= (10 \times 5)$ mg $\times$ mg $= 50$ mg^2 (50 mg squared)

x)   10 mg $\div$ 5 $= (10 \div 5)$ mg $= 2$ mg

xi)   10 mg $\div$ 5 mg $= (10 \div 5)$ mg $\div$ mg $= 2$ (no units)

xii) 10 $\div$ 5 mg $= (10 \div 5)$ $\div$ mg $= 2 \div$ mg $= 2$/mg (2 per mg)

Note how the units in examples vii) and xi) have been cancelled out (eliminated). In example x) we can change 'dividing by 5' to 'multiplying by one-fifth', to remove the division sign. It is useful to know how to do this because *it is easier to work with equations that contain only multiplication signs*.

Example x) becomes $10 \text{ mg} \div 5 = 10 \times \dfrac{1}{5} \text{ mg} = \dfrac{10}{5} \text{ mg} = 2 \text{ mg}$

Alternatively, the 5 can be placed directly below the 10 so that we can omit the multiplication sign, as shown for example xi) below.

Example xi) becomes $10 \text{ mg} \div 5 \text{ mg} = \dfrac{10 \text{ mg}}{5 \text{ mg}} = 2$ (no units)

In the above example the mg units can be seen to cancel each other out. Alternatively, you could replace mg/mg with $\times 1$ as in:

$$10 \text{ mg} \div 5 \text{ mg} = \dfrac{10 \text{ mg}}{5 \text{ mg}} = 2 \times 1 = 2 \text{ (no units)}$$

In example xii) we are dividing by mg, so it appears beneath the number 2 as in $\dfrac{2}{\text{mg}}$ (two per mg; or 2 mg^{-1} in scientific notation).

The rest of this section explains how you make drug calculations without using an equation, by cancelling the units. The answers have the units ml, ml per hour, or drops per minute.

Example 1
The prescription states 300 mg (milligrams). Stock ampoules are 500 mg in 4 ml. How much do you give?

Answer: In this question, 'How much do you give?' means how many ml, so whatever calculation you do, *it must end with an answer having the units ml*.

1) Start with the prescription: 300 mg

2) Look what you've got: 500 mg in 4 ml (that is to say, 500 mg per 4 ml, which can be written as 500 mg/4 ml or as 500 mg divided by 4 ml, which is $\dfrac{500 \text{ mg}}{4 \text{ ml}}$)

3) Summarize the information in the question as follows, making sure to include all the units:

i)   300 mg   ii) $\dfrac{500 \text{ mg}}{4 \text{ ml}}$

4) We want an answer in ml. How can we get this? Look at the ml units in ii). They appear *beneath* the 500 mg term. This is no use. *The ml needs to be on the top for an answer ending in ml.* So we need to turn the number (with its units) upside down:

ii) $\dfrac{500 \text{ mg}}{\textbf{4 ml}}$ becomes $\dfrac{\textbf{4 ml}}{500 \text{ mg}}$

5) Multiply the prescription in i) by the upside down (inverted) number as it appears above, remembering to keep the units in place.

$$300 \text{ mg} \times \frac{4 \text{ ml}}{500 \text{ mg}}$$

6) Cross-cancel the mg at the top with the mg at the bottom ('cancel out' the mg units); or if you prefer mg/mg = × 1

7) This leaves us with $300 \times \dfrac{4 \text{ ml}}{500}$, ie $3 \times \dfrac{4 \text{ ml}}{5}$
(cross-cancelling the double zeros or dividing the top and bottom by 100 if you prefer) $= \dfrac{12 \text{ ml}}{5} = 2.4 \text{ ml}$

The two key steps needed to reach the answer without reference to an equation were:

i)   write the prescription and the stock: 300 mg and $\dfrac{500 \text{ mg}}{4 \text{ ml}}$

ii) multiply the prescription by the stock rewritten so that the ml units appear at the top with the mg units at the bottom:

$300 \text{ mg} \times \dfrac{4 \text{ ml}}{500 \text{ mg}}$ (then cancel out the mg units top and bottom)

Check your answer by working the question backwards starting with the answer. Ask yourself how much medication is there in 2.4 ml. We have 500 mg in 4 ml, which means there is 125 mg in 1 ml.

Working out how much medication (mg) you have in 1 ml is known as the *unitary* method. It helps to break down the arithmetic into manageable steps.

We have 2.4 ml, which can be split into 2 ml + 0.4 ml for convenience and then multiplied by 125 mg (the number of milligrams in 1 ml): $2 \times 125 + 0.4 \times 125 = 2 \times 125 + 4 \times 12.5$ (multiplying the 0.4 by 10 and dividing 125 by 10, 'to balance the books'). Multiplying and recombining (adding) the quantities give: 250 mg + 50 mg = 300 mg, as stated in the prescription.

Example 2

The patient weighs 60 kg. The prescription orders an injection of 3 mg/kg and the medication is available in 2 ml vials containing 100 mg. How much do you draw up?

1) The prescription requires 3 mg/kg (3 mg per kg)

2) We have 100 mg in 2 ml or 100 mg/2 ml

3) Write 1) and 2) as: $\dfrac{3\,mg}{kg}$ and $\dfrac{100\,mg}{2\,ml}$

4) Look where the ml units are because these will need to appear on the top line with the remaining units (mg and kg) cancelled out because we only want ml in the answer.
   So we invert the second term and write:

$$\frac{3\,mg}{kg} \times \frac{2\,ml}{100\,mg} \times 60\,kg$$

5) Cross-cancel the two mg units and the two kg units, top and bottom, to leave $\dfrac{3 \times 2\,ml \times 60}{100}$ to give $\dfrac{360\,ml}{100} = 3.6\,ml$
   Notice that the three top terms (3, 2 ml and 60) have been brought together on a single line for a neater look, rather than appearing as separate terms.

Check your answer by working the question backwards, starting with the answer. Ask yourself how much medication is there in 3.6 ml. If a 2 ml vial contains 100 mg, then 1 ml will contain half as much or 50 mg, and 3.6 ml will contain (by splitting 3.6 into 3 and 0.6): 3.6 × 50 mg = 3 × 50 mg + 0.6 × 50 mg = 150 mg + 30 mg = 180 mg. For a patient weighing 60 kg, this dose will be equal to 3 mg per kg, as ordered by the prescription.

Example 3
The script states 100 micrograms/kg/minute. You have 200 mg in 50 ml. If the patient weighs 80 kg, at what rate (ml/hr) do you set the pump?

We have: $\dfrac{100 \text{ microg}}{\text{kg minute}}$ $\dfrac{200 \text{ mg}}{50 \text{ ml}}$ 80 kg

Convert 100 micrograms to milligrams as a first step. In the second term place the 50 ml at the top with the 200 mg below it because ml must appear on the top line.

So: $\dfrac{0.1 \text{ mg}}{\text{kg min}}$ $\times$ $\dfrac{50 \text{ ml}}{200 \text{ mg}}$ $\times$ 80 kg

Cancelling the mg and kg terms leaves us with

$$\frac{0.1}{\text{min}} \times \frac{50 \text{ ml}}{200} \times 80 = \frac{0.1 \times 5 \times 8}{2} \frac{\text{ml}}{\text{min}} = \frac{4 \text{ ml}}{2 \text{ min}} = \frac{2 \text{ ml}}{\text{min}}$$

Note that the time term (minute) is at the bottom, where it needs to be. However, we want ml per hour. It is easy to see that 2 ml/minute is 120 ml/hour. However, the units can be used to guide this extra step if necessary. We want an answer in ml/hr.

This means that we *need ml at the top with hr at the bottom and mins cancelled out*. To achieve this end we need to *multiply by* the units min per hour (min/hr).

$$\frac{2 \text{ ml}}{\text{min}} \frac{\text{min}}{\text{hr}}$$

There are 60 minutes per hour, so we can write

$$\frac{2 \text{ ml}}{\text{min}} \times \frac{60 \text{ min}}{\text{hr}} = 120 \text{ ml/hr (after cross-cancelling the mins)}$$

Check your answer by working the question backwards, noting that 120 ml/hr = 2 ml/minute. Ask yourself how much medication is there in 2 ml. The question indicates that there are 200 mg in 50 ml, so dividing both quantities by 50 (cancelling by 50) gives 4 mg in 1 ml (per minute), which is 8 mg (8000 micrograms) in 2 ml (per minute). The patient weighs 80 kg, so 8000 micrograms per minute is equivalent 100 micrograms per kilogram per minute, as stated in the script.

Example 4

In this example we will look at what happens to the units when a calculation goes wrong.

A patient is prescribed 5 mg of diazepam. Stock is 2 mg/5 ml syrup. You do a quick mental calculation and decide that that the patient requires 2 ml.

You worked this out at follows: $5 \times 2/5 = 10/5 = 2$ ml.

With the units in place: $5 \text{ mg} \times \dfrac{2 \text{ mg}}{5 \text{ ml}} = \dfrac{10}{5} \dfrac{\text{mg} \times \text{mg}}{\text{ml}} = 2 \text{ mg}^2/\text{ml}$

An answer with the wrong units must have the wrong numbers.

Using the units to guide the process gives:

5 mg prescribed; stock is 2 mg/5 ml or $\dfrac{2 \text{ mg}}{5 \text{ ml}}$

$5 \text{ mg} \times \dfrac{5 \text{ ml}}{2 \text{ mg}} = 5 \times \dfrac{5}{2} \text{ ml} = \dfrac{25 \text{ ml}}{2} = 12.5$ ml (units are correct)

An answer with the right units will not necessarily have the right numbers, so work the calculation in reverse to check it.

Ask yourself how much medication there is in 12.5 ml. Stock is 2 mg in every 5 ml and we have 12.5 ml. Calculate how much medication there is in 1 ml (the unitary method), as a first step, as follows.

5 ml contains 2 mg, so 1 ml contains $1/5 \times 2$ mg $= 2/5$ mg $= 4/10$ mg $= 0.4$ mg; then 12.5 ml contains 12.5×0.4 mg $= 1.25 \times 4$ (multiplying the 0.4 by 10 and dividing 12.5 by 10, 'to balance the books') to give 5 ml, ie correct. In this example, a better method would have been to split the 12.5 ml into convenient packets of 5 ml and 2.5 ml, where every 5 ml contains 2 mg and every 2.5 ml contains 1 mg.

12.5 ml = 5 ml + 5 ml + 2.5 ml, ie 2 mg + 2 mg + 1 mg = 5 mg

Example 5 (see Test 47, question 1e)

The treatment is a continuous intravenous infusion of dopamine. You have 400 mg of the drug, ready mixed in 250 ml of 5% glucose infusion fluid. The rate of the infusion is to be 3 micrograms/kg/minute and the patient weighs 89 kg. Calculate the infusion rate in ml/hr. We have:

$$\frac{400 \text{ mg}}{250 \text{ ml}} \qquad \frac{3 \text{ microg}}{\text{kg min}} \qquad 89 \text{ kg}$$

We want ml/hr, so the first term (not the second term the way the information is written) needs to be inverted to get the ml units on the top. So we have:

$$\frac{250 \text{ ml}}{400 \text{ mg}} \times \frac{3 \text{ microg}}{\text{kg min}} \times 89 \text{ kg}$$

At this stage it is normal to convert the 3 micrograms in the second term to milligrams (equally we could convert 400 mg in the first term to micrograms, for the same effect). However, a dimensional analysis tells us that we do not want micrograms or milligrams in the answer, so we need to cancel out both of these units. This is done by multiplying by mg and dividing by micrograms, ie

$$\frac{\text{milligram}}{\text{microgram}}$$

There are 1000 micrograms in 1 mg, so multiply by $\dfrac{1 \text{ mg}}{1000 \text{ microg}}$

to give: $\dfrac{250 \text{ ml}}{400 \text{ mg}} \times \dfrac{3 \text{ microg}}{\text{kg min}} \times \dfrac{1 \text{ mg}}{1000 \text{ microg}} \times 89 \text{ kg}$

Cancelling all the units for weight leaves

$$\frac{250 \text{ ml}}{400} \times \frac{3}{\text{min}} \times \frac{1}{1000} \times 89$$

The infusion rate per hour is 60 times that per minute and is given by

$$\frac{250 \text{ ml}}{400} \times \frac{3}{\text{min}} \times \frac{1}{1000} \times 89 \times 60 \frac{\text{min}}{\text{hr}}$$

Cancelling the minutes top and bottom, the two zeros top and bottom (cancelling by 10 once then once again) and dividing by 5 top and bottom (cancelling by 5 once and then once again) gives:

$$\frac{5 \text{ ml} \times 3 \times 89 \times 6}{8 \times 100 \times hr} = \frac{5 \times 18 \times 89}{800} \text{ ml/h}$$

Work this out using a calculator or simplify it a step further first to give:

$$\frac{89 \times 9}{80} \text{ ml/hr} = 10.0 \text{ ml/hr (on a calculator)}$$

Check your answer by working the question backwards starting with the answer. Ask yourself what the infusion rate is in micrograms/kg/minute for a flow rate of 10.0 ml/hr.

10 ml per hour is 10/250 × 400 mg per hour = 4000/250 = 16000/1000 (multiplying top and bottom by 4 converts the 250 to 1000 making the division step much easier) = 16 mg/hr

16 mg/hour = 16 × 1000 microg × 1/60 min = 1600/6 = 800/3 = 266.67 microg./min (on a calculator); dividing by 89 kg (per kg) gives 3.0 micrograms/kg/minute, which is stated in the script.

Calculating the infusion rate with 'dimensional analysis' is easier than using the step-by-step method shown in Test 47 question 1e (and expanded on in the answer section).

Example 6 (see question 16, end of Chapter 4)

One litre of physiological saline (0.9% w/v) is to be given over 6 hours with a 20 drop per ml giving set. What is the drop rate in drops per minute (to the nearest drop)?

In this example we treat 'drop' the same way as any other unit because it is a *quantity* with the dimensions of volume. This means that we can use 'dimensional analysis' with questions that refer to drops.

We have 1 litre per 6 hours and 20 drops per ml. We express this mathematically as per the previous examples

$$\frac{1\,L}{6\,hr} \qquad \frac{20\,drops}{ml}$$

We want an answer in drops per minute ie drop/min or $\dfrac{drop}{min}$

We have 'drop' on the top line, where it needs to be, but we need to convert hours to minutes and cancel out the litre and ml units after converting one unit to the other, ie

$$\frac{1\,L}{6\,hr} \times \frac{1\,hr}{60\,min} \times \frac{1000\,ml}{1\,L} \times \frac{20\,drop}{ml}$$

These units will now cancel correctly to leave drop/min:

$$\frac{1000 \times 20}{6 \times 60}\frac{drop}{min} = \frac{1000}{6 \times 3}\,drop/min = \frac{500}{9}\,dpm = 55.56\,dpm$$

ie *56 dpm to the nearest drop*

Check your answer by working the question backwards starting with the answer. It is not necessary to start with the exact answer when checking it. We can use an approximate value to make the working out easier. In this case we can round up 56 dpm to the nearest 10, ie to 60 dpm.

A drop is a unit of volume. There are 20 drops per ml, so one drop is one-twentieth of a ml (1/20 ml or 0.05 ml).

Staying with fractions rather than decimals, we convert 60 dpm to ml per hour

There are 20 drops in every 1 ml, so 60 drops $= 60 \times \dfrac{1}{20} = 3$ ml

ie 60 dpm = 3 ml/minute = 3 × 60 ml/hr = 180 ml/hr, which gives 6 × 180 ml/hr = 1080 ml after 6 hours (1.08 L). This answer is slightly higher than the one litre ordered by the prescription, and is consistent with the approximation we chose.

A full dimensional analysis of this checking method would be:

$$60 \, \frac{\text{drops}}{\text{min}} \qquad \frac{20 \text{ drops}}{\text{ml}}$$

$$60 \, \frac{\text{drops}}{\text{min}} \times 60 \, \frac{\text{min}}{\text{hr}} \times \frac{1 \text{ ml}}{20 \text{ drops}}$$

Cancelling the drops and the minutes leaves

$$\frac{60 \times 60}{20} \, \frac{\text{ml}}{\text{hr}} = 180 \text{ ml/hr (or 1080 ml after 6 hours)}$$

Example 7
A patient is prescribed 1 g of paracetamol and the stock is 500 mg tablets. How many tablets do you give?

It is obvious that the answer is two tablets, but it is worth looking at how dimensional analysis tackles the question.

We have: 1 g prescribed and 500 mg tablets. To avoid decimal numbers (in this example 0.5 g) we convert grams to milligrams (using dimensional analysis). We also write 500 mg tablets (500 mg per tablet) as 500 mg/tablet or rather $\frac{500 \text{ mg}}{\text{tablet}}$

So we have: $1 \text{ g} \quad 1000 \, \frac{\text{mg}}{\text{g}} \quad \frac{500 \text{ mg}}{\text{tablet}}$

We need tablet to appear on the top line on its own, so we invert the last term to give

$$1 \text{ g} \times 1000 \, \frac{\text{mg}}{\text{g}} \times \frac{\text{tablet}}{500 \text{ mg}}$$

Cross-cancelling the gram units and the milligram units leaves

$$\frac{1000}{500} \text{ tablet} = 2 \text{ tablets}$$

Abbreviations

Instructions for the administration of drugs are best written out in full in English without abbreviation. However, a lack of space on drug charts means that some abbreviations find widespread use. Most are easily understood except for a few in Latin that need to be remembered. The following abbreviations may be used in some tests and you will see them on patients' drug charts.

p.o., PO or O = orally
i/v or IV = intravenous injection; IVI = intravenous infusion
i/m or IM = intramuscular injection
s/c or SC = subcutaneous injection
s/l or SL = sublingually (easily confused with SC)
p.r. or PR = into the rectum
p.v. or PV = into the vagina
top or TOP = topically
inh or INH = inhaled
neb or NEB = nebulized
NG = via nasogastric tube
PEG = via percutaneous endoscopic gastrostomy (PEG) tube

The following Latin abbreviations still find use although English words are preferred. Most refer to the frequency and time of drug administration. It is not a comprehensive list.

prn or PRN = when required
stat or STAT = at once
o.d. (OD) = once daily
b.d. (BD) or b.i.d. (BID) = twice daily
t.d.s. (TDS) or t.i.d. (TID) = three times daily
q.d.s. (QDS) or q.i.d. (QID) = four times daily
(In the United States QD = once daily)
o.m. or mane = in the morning
o.n. or nocte = at night
a.c = before meals
p.c. = after meals
q = each/every
h = hourly

The following English abbreviations find widespread use:

1/7 = for one day; 1/12 for one month; 1/52 for one week
2/7 = for two days; 2/12 for two months; 2/52 for two weeks etc
1^0 = hourly; 2^0 = two hourly etc.
1 tablet = Ť   2 tablets = ŤŤ

Prescription awareness

As a nurse you will encounter drugs and drug administration situations that you are not familiar with. Most difficulties can be solved by referring to an up-to-date issue of the British National Formulary (the BNF handbook) or by consulting another nurse or a doctor. The following questions and answers will help address some of the more common dilemmas that arise.

1 The patient is prescribed an oral solution of morphine sulphate 10–20 mg for post-operative analgesia. The patient is complaining of pain and you administer two 5 ml vials each containing 10 mg of morphine sulphate. Correct or incorrect?

Incorrect: start with the lowest dose. (If the pain is unrelieved the remainder can be given.)

2 The patient is prescribed paracetamol 0.5–1 g every 4 to 6 hours prn to a maximum of 4 g daily. You give the patient 1 g at 0800 hrs. The patient requests a further dose at midday but you ask the patient to wait until 2 pm. Correct or incorrect?

Incorrect: the dose can be given every four hours at the patient's request (to a maximum of 4 g daily).

3 The patient is prescribed 1 g of co-codamol prn and is complaining of pain. You have 30/500 tablets and administer two of these. Correct or incorrect?

Incorrect: You have made a drug administration error. Always give the lower strength 8/500 co-codamol tablets where no strength is specified.

4 The patient is prescribed aspirin for pain relief. You have two strengths of tablet, 75 mg and 300 mg. You administer one 300 mg tablet. Correct or incorrect?

Correct: The standard dose is one 300 mg tablet when no dose is stated.

Test 50

1 A patient is prescribed warfarin 6 mg o.d. Stock is 3 mg tablets. How many tablets will the patient receive in a two-day period?

2 The patient is prescribed sodium valproate 200 mg b.d. How many milligrams will be given to the patient in a 24-hour period?

3 A patient is taking amoxicillin 500 mg t.d.s. How many grams of amoxicillin will the patient consume in total if the treatment lasts five days?

4 The patient is written up for paracetamol 1 g q.d.s. What is the total daily dose?

5 A patient is written up for furosemide 20 mg i/m. How many 20 mg tablets will be given to the patient in 24 hours? (trick question)

6 The prescription is 20 ml lactulose b.d. How many full days supply of lactulose are there in a 500 ml bottle?

7 The patient is written up for haloperidol 0.5–1.5 gram o.d. or b.d. prn. What is the maximum daily dose?

8 The prescription states bisacodyl 10 mg 1 tablet p.o. b.i.d. How many milligrams of bisacodyl should the patient take each day?

9 A patient is written up for cyclizine 50 mg/ml s/c 4°. How many 1 ml ampoules will be required for a 24-hour period?

10 The treatment is lansoprazole 30 mg o.m. for 8 weeks. Stock is 15 mg tablets. How many 28-capsule packs are required for the full treatment?

11 The patient is taking 2.5 mg of dexamethasone q.d.s. for 5 days. Stock tablets are 500 micrograms and 2 mg. How many dexamethasone tablets will be dispensed over the five-day period?

12 Diamorphine 5 mg i/m q4 hrs is prescribed. How many milli-grams is this daily?

Drug familiarity

The most time-consuming part of any drug round is finding the right medication in the drug trolley. This problem has eased with the use of patients' own drugs (PODs) kept in bedside cabinets. However, not all patients have their own drugs or a secure place to store them, so the ward drug trolley still finds widespread use. Finding medication improves quickly with practice, especially if the trolley is kept tidy, with the drugs arranged in alphabetical order.

The majority of drugs are prescribed by their approved (generic) name and not by the manufacturers' (brand) name. The brand name usually takes precedence on the packaging, with the approved name written in small print underneath. For this reason a good know-ledge of brand names is an advantage in drug administration.

If a nurse informed you that she had given a patient two Panadols®, what would this mean to you? Would you need to refer to the BNF handbook to find out she meant one gram of paracetamol? Examples of some common medications and their brand names are shown in Table 5.1. You will find a list like this helpful in locating patients' medications in the drug trolley. Some of the drugs have more than one brand name but only one name has been included in the list. Read through it carefully and slowly, then complete the test.

Patients often have little insight into their medications. A patient on Kapake® (co-codamol 30/500), for example, might not even realize it contains paracetamol. However, you should have a basic idea of a drug's purpose (indication) before administering it: for example analgesic, anti-emetic, anti-hypertensive, anti-depressant, antibiotic. This information is beyond the scope of this book but is available in the BNF handbook.

TABLE 5.1 Approved and brand names of common drugs

Approved name	Brand name	Approved name	Brand name	Approved name	Brand name
Acetylcysteine	Parvolex®	Darbepoetin alfa	Aranesp®	Nicorandil	Ikorel®
Aciclovir	Zovirax®	Diazepam	Valium®	Nalaxone	Narcan®
Alendronic acid	Fosamax®	Dicolfenac	Voltarol®	Omeprazole	Losec®
Alfuzosin	Xatral®	Dipyridamole	Persantin®	Pancreatin	Creon®
Amisulpride	Solian®	Disulfiram	Antabuse®	Pantoprazole	Protium®
Atrovastatin	Lipitor®	Donepezil	Aricept®	Paroxetine	Seroxat®
Baclofen	Lioresal®	Domperidone	Motilium®	Potassium chloride	Sando-K®
Beclometasone	Becotide®	Enoxaparin	Clexane®	Pramipexole	Mirapexin®
Betahistine	Serc®	Entanercept	Enbrel®	Perindropil	Coversyl®
Bisoprolol	Cardicor®	Etoricoxib	Arcoxia®	Prochlorperazine	Stemetil®
Budesonide	Symbicort®	Fluoxetine	Prozac®	Quetiapine	Serequel®
Carbamazepine	Tegretol®	Furosemide	Lasix®	Ranitidine	Zantac®
Ceftriaxone	Rocephin®	Haloperidol	Serenace®	Risedronate	Actonel®
Chlordiazepoxide	Librium®	Hydrocortisone	Solu-Cortef®	Rivastigmine	Exelon®
Chlorpromazine	Largactil®	Hyoscine butylbromide	Buscopan®	Ropinirole	Requip®
Chlorphenamine	Piriton®	Ibuprofen	Brufen®	Rosiglitazone	Avandia®
Ciprofloxacin	Ciproxin®	Insulin glargine	Lantus®	Salbutamol	Ventolin®
Citalopram	Cipramil®	Ipratropium bromide	Atrovent®	Salmeterol	Serevent®
Clarithromycin	Klaricid®	Lansoprazole	Zoton®	Senna	Senokot®
Clopidogrel	Plavix®	Lercanidipine	Zanidip®	Silver sulfadiazine	Flamazine®
Co-amoxiclav	Augmentin®	Levomepromazine	Nozinan®	Sodium valproate	Epilim®
Co-beneldopa	Mopar®	Meloxicam	Mobic®	Tamsulosin	Flomax®
Co-careldopa	Sinemet®	Metoclopramide	Maxolon®	Thiamine	Pabrinex®
Co-codamol(30/500)	Kapake®	Metrondiazole	Flagyl®	Tiotropium bromide	Spiriva®
Cyclizine	Valoid®	Midazolam	Hypnovel®	Tolterodine tartrate	Detrusitol®
Danaparoid	Organan®	Mirtazapine	Zispin®	Zopiclone	Zimovane®

Test 51

Check your knowledge of brand names by choosing the correct brand from A, B or C for the prescription shown.

	Prescription	Brand A, B or C?	Answer
1	Ibuprofen	A. Panadol® B. Brufen® C. Kapake®	
2	Ciprofloxacin	A. Ciproxin® B. Cipramil® C. Clinoril®	
3	Citalopram	A. Molipaxin® B. Caprilon® C. Cipramil®	
4	Aciclover	A. Zovirax® B. Zanidip® C. Zantac®	
5	Metrondiazole	A. Nysran® B. Flagyl® C. Zovirax®	
6	Insulin glargine	A. Mixtard® B. Humulin® C. Lantus®	
7	Enoxaparin	A. Clexane® B. Orgaran® C. Hepsal®	
8	Isorbide mononitrite	A. Monomax® B. Flomax® C. Lasix®	

	Prescription	Brand A, B or C?	Answer
9	Lansoprazole	A. Losec® B. Protium® C. Zoton®	
10	Cyclizine	A. Serc® B. Valoid® C. Buscopan®	
11	Diclofenac	A. Voltarol® B. Aricept® C. Nozinan®	
12	Valproate	A. Epilim® B. Creon® C. Enbrel®	
13	Ranitidine	A. Zanidip® B. Losec® C. Zantac®	
14	Metoclopramide	A. Valoid® B. Persantin® C. Maxolon®	
15	Budesonide	A. Ventolin® B. Serevent® C. Symbicort®	
16	Perindopril	A. Actonel® B. Coversyl® C. Ikorel®	
17	Carbamazepine	A. Tegretol® B. Detrusitol® C. Exelon®	

	Prescription	Brand A, B or C?	Answer
18	Bisoprolol	A. Cardicor® B. Sinemet® C. Xatral®	
19	Clopidrogel	A. Lasix® B. Plavix® C. Pabrinex®	
20	Co-amoxiclav	A. Rocephin® B. Augmentin® C. Ceporex®	

Test 52

Refer to the container labels on the next two pages to answer the following questions.

1   The treatment is an intravenous infusion of ciprofloxacin, 400 mg b.d. given over 1 hour. What is the infusion rate in ml/hour?

2   The patient takes 30 mg of balcofen daily in three divided doses. How many 5 ml spoonfuls will you administer per dose?

3   An injection of enoxaparin is required. The dose is 0.5 mg per kg and the patient weighs 60 kg. What volume of enoxaparin must be expelled from the pre-filled syringe 100 mg/ml before the injection can be given?

4   The treatment is an intravenous infusion of imipenem with cilastatin. 1.5 g is to be given daily in three divided doses. How many vials will be needed each day?

5   The patient needs a 20 mg bolus dose of Maxolon® to be given by intravenous injection. What will you draw up?

6   The client takes 20 mg of Prozac® each day. Exactly what will you measure out?

7   The treatment sheet shows that 'four 5 ml spoonfuls of carbamazepine' are to be administered. How many milligrams of the drug is this?

8   The treatment sheet reads GTN s/l prn. What does the patient need to be given?

Clexane® Syringes

enoxaparin sodium

Solution for Injection

10 x **0.4** ml Pre-filled syringes   ✳*Aventis*

Starter pack 4.9 g

Nitrolingual® P U M P S P R A Y

Each metered dose of sublingual spray contains 400 micrograms glyceryl trinitrate.
Adults & elderly Spray 1 or 2 metered doses under the tongue.
No more than 3 metered doses at a time. Children: not recommended.

Liquid   5 mg/5 ml

Baclofen Ph.Eur.

To be taken by mouth

POM

500 mg Monovial pack **PRIMAXIN® IV 500 mg**
(imipenem/cilastatin sodium)
Powder for solution for infusion
For intravenous use
single vial pack

Infusion

Ciprofloxacin 400 mg/200 ml

1 infusion
vial of **400mg**
ciprofloxacin/
200ml

POM

For intravenous
administration
by infusion

ESSENTIAL GENERICS

Fluoxetine

20 mg/5 ml

Oral Solution

Sugar Free

70 ml

Metoclopramide
Injection

10 mg in 2 ml

10 mg in 2 ml

10 ampoules each containing 2 ml
solution for i.m. or i.v. injection.

Liquid 100 mg/5 ml

Carbamazepine Ph.Eur.

To be taken by mouth

How to read tables and drug charts

Drug charts, also referred to as 'treatment sheets' or 'MAR sheets' (medication administration records), display drug dosage information laid out in tables. Tabulated data is arranged in columns and rows. A simple table is shown below. It has two columns and seven rows. To find a piece of information you read down a column and across a row.

Percentage losses of vitamins in vegetables during cooking

Vitamin			% losses
Carotene (D)			0
Thiamine (B1)			40
Riboflavin (B2)			40
Vitamin C			70
Vitamin E			0
Vitamin B6			40
Folic Acid			90

Questions
1. How much vitamin C is lost by cooking?   Answer: 70%
2. How much folic acid is lost by cooking?   Answer: 90%

The method of finding information on treatment sheets is similar. You look down a column and across a row to find the answer. The columns are the days of the month (1 to 31). The rows are the times of administration. There are typically four rows corresponding to morning, midday, evening and bedtime.

So you need to read *along* the row corresponding to the time of day, then *down* the column that is headed by the date of the month you are at (1 to 31). This date should have already been entered if the morning drugs have been administered, otherwise you will need to enter it in the correct column, next to the previous day's date.

Treatment sheet questions

This section tests your ability to read drug dosage charts (treatment sheets). Study the charts carefully or the questions may catch you out. In practice, how long you take to complete the drug round is far less important than the need to avoid making a mistake.

Key point: drug charts are much easier to read once you have identified the correct time of day and the correct date.

Key point: when a drug has been administered there should be a signature to identify who gave it, at what time and on what day.

Example

Using first sample treatment sheet shown (sample A), decide whether the statements written below are true or false.

1   The patient's name is Stephen Williams.

TRUE/FALSE

2   15 ml of lactulose are to be administered in the morning and again in the evening.

TRUE/FALSE

3   You have atentolol 25 mg stock and should administer two tablets in the morning.

TRUE/FALSE

4   You should give the patient one 40 mg tablet of furosemide in the morning.

TRUE/FALSE

Explanation of answers

1   True, the name is correct (and in practice you have checked it against the patient).

2   True, the right dose given at the right times.

3   False, the doctor has not signed the sheet. Do not give it.

4   False, the correct route for administering the drug is i.m.

MEDICATION ADMINISTRATION RECORD – sample A
PATIENTS NAME: STEPHEN WILLIAMS

ROUTE	*p.o.*	MEDICINE						DR's SIGNATURE					
DATE	1st Feb	*Lactulose*						*PS Brown*					
	DOSE	1	2	3	4	5	6	7	8	9	10	11	12
Morning	15 ml												
Midday													
Evening	15 ml												
Bedtime													

ROUTE	*p.o.*	MEDICINE						DR's SIGNATURE					
DATE	1st Feb	*Atenolol*											
	DOSE	1	2	3	4	5	6	7	8	9	10	11	12
Morning	50 mg												
Midday													
Evening													
Bedtime													

ROUTE	*i.m.*	MEDICINE						DR's SIGNATURE					
DATE	1st Feb	*Furosemide*						*PS Brown*					
	DOSE	1	2	3	4	5	6	7	8	9	10	11	12
Morning	40 mg												
Midday													
Evening													
Bedtime													

Test 53

Using the second sample treatment sheet shown (sample B), decide whether the statements written below are true or false. The boxes on the treatment sheet with a nurse's signature inside show which nurse has administered the drug and at what time of day.

1   The patient's name is Christopher Johns.

TRUE/FALSE

2   The patient has been prescribed 4 g of paracetamol daily.

TRUE/FALSE

3   The patient's next dose of omeprazole will be one 20 mg capsule, which is due on 3 May in the morning.

TRUE/FALSE

4   The patient's next dose of paracetamol is two 500 mg tablets to be given in the morning of 3 May.

TRUE/FALSE

5   The patient is written up for perindopril. The stock is 4 mg tablets. It is 8 am on 3 May so you should administer ten 4 mg tablets.

TRUE/FALSE

MEDICATION ADMINISTRATION RECORD – sample B
PATIENT'S NAME: CHRISTOPHER JOHNSON

ROUTE	*p.o.*	MEDICINE						DR's SIGNATURE					
DATE	1/5	*Paracetamol*						*M Aziz*					
	DOSE	1	2	3	4	5	6	7	8	9	10	11	12
Morning	1g	KS	CR	CR									
Midday	1g	CR	KS										
Evening	1g	CR	CR										
Bedtime	1g	BI	BI										

ROUTE	*p.o.*	MEDICINE						DR's SIGNATURE					
DATE	1/5	*Omeprazole*						*M Aziz*					
	DOSE	1	2	3	4	5	6	7	8	9	10	11	12
Morning	20 mg	KS	CR										
Midday													
Evening													
Bedtime													

ROUTE	*p.o.*	MEDICINE						DR's SIGNATURE					
DATE	1/5	*Perindopril*						*M Aziz*					
	DOSE	1	2	3	4	5	6	7	8	9	10	11	12
Morning	40 mg	KS	CR										
Midday													
Evening													
Bedtime													

Test 54

Using the third sample treatment sheet (sample C), decide whether the statements written below are true or false.

1 The patient's name is Mary Roberts.

TRUE/FALSE

2 Twenty milligram of levothyroxine has been prescribed and it should be administered first thing in the morning.

TRUE/FALSE

3 The patient is taking 150 mg of diclofenac per day.

TRUE/FALSE

4 You have diclofenac in stock as 25 mg tablets. It is 0800 hrs on 10 June so the patient is due three tablets.

TRUE/FALSE

5 At midday on 10 June Mrs Roberts complains of pain so you can administer the evening dose of diclofenac at lunchtime.

TRUE/FALSE

6 Mrs Roberts may not have received her 40 mg of gliclazide on the evening of 9 June.

TRUE/FALSE

MEDICATION ADMINISTRATION RECORD – sample C
PATIENT'S NAME: MARY ROBERTS

ROUTE	*p.o.*	MEDICINE						DR's SIGNATURE					
DATE	5/6	*Levothyroxine*						*A Ahmed*					
	DOSE	5	6	7	8	9	10	11	12	13	14	15	16
Morning	20 mcg	KS	CR	BI	Is	CR	CR						
Midday													
Evening													
Bedtime													

ROUTE	*p.o.*	MEDICINE						DR's SIGNATURE					
DATE	5/6	*Diclofenac*						*A Ahmed*					
	DOSE	5	6	7	8	9	10	11	12	13	14	15	16
Morning	75 mg	KS	CR	BI	KS	CR	CR						
Midday													
Evening	75 mg	KS	CR	BI	KS	CR							
Bedtime													

ROUTE	*p.o.*	MEDICINE						DR's SIGNATURE					
DATE	5/6	*Gliclazide*						*A Ahmed*					
	DOSE	5	6	7	8	9	10	11	12	13	14	15	16
Morning	40 mg	KS	CR	BI	KS	CR	CR						
Midday													
Evening	40 mg	KS	CR	BI	KS								
Bedtime													

Test 55

Using the fourth sample treatment sheet (sample D), decide whether the statements written below are true or false. You may need to refer to the code at the bottom of the treatment sheet to answer some of the questions.

1   The patient's name is Ifan Griffiths.

TRUE/FALSE

2   Over a 24-hour period on 1 July the patient took a total of eight tablets of 8/500 strength co-codamol.

TRUE/FALSE

3   Over a 24-hour period on 2 July 2nd the patient took a total of eight tablets of co-codamol of 30/500 strength.

TRUE/FALSE

4   If each 30/500 co-codamol tablet contains 30 mg of codeine phosphate together with 500 mg of paracetamol, then on the first day of the month Mr Griffiths took a total of 4 g of paracetamol and 0.24 g of codeine phosphate.

TRUE/FALSE

5   Amoxicillin was not available until the evening of 3 July.

TRUE/FALSE

6   The warfarin dose varies from day to day and is shown on a separate chart. The next dose is 7 milligrams. Tablets come in strengths of 0.5, 1, 3 and 5 mg. The minimum number of warfarin tablets to be administered on the evening of 6 July is three.

TRUE/FALSE

MEDICATION ADMINISTRATION RECORD – sample D
PATIENT'S NAME: IFAN GRIFFITHS

ROUTE	*p.o.*	MEDICINE						DR's SIGNATURE					
DATE	1/7	*Co-codamol 30/500*						*A Ahmed*					
	DOSE	1	2	3	4	5	6	7	8	9	10	11	12
Morning	Two	KS	4	BI	KS	CR	CR						
Midday	Two	KS	4	BI	KS	CR							
Evening	Two	KS	CR	BI	KS	CR							
Bedtime	Two	TD	TD	TD	CJ	CJ							

ROUTE	*p.o.*	MEDICINE						DR's SIGNATURE					
DATE	1/7	*Amoxycillin*						*A Ahmed*					
	DOSE	1	2	3	4	5	6	7	8	9	10	11	12
Morning	250 mg	5	5	5	KS	CR	CR						
Midday													
Evening	250 mg	5	5	BI	KS	CR							
Bedtime													

ROUTE	*p.o.*	MEDICINE						DR's SIGNATURE					
DATE	1/7	*Warfarin*						*A Ahmed*					
	DOSE	1	2	3	4	5	6	7	8	9	10	11	12
Morning													
Midday													
Evening	as chart	KS	CR	BI	KS	CR							
Bedtime													

Non administration codes: 4 = refused; 5 = medication unavailable

Test 56

Using the fifth sample treatment sheet, (sample E), decide whether the statements written below are true or false. You may need to refer to the code at the bottom of the treatment sheet to answer some of the questions.

1   James McMahon takes 15 microgram of lansoprazole in the morning.

TRUE/FALSE

2   He was written up for 0.4 g of dipyridamole daily.

TRUE/FALSE

3   The patient refused to take his dipyridamole on the morning of 5 August and has not taken any since.

TRUE/FALSE

4   The total amount of dipyridamole administered to Mr McMahon this month is 1.8 g.

TRUE/FALSE

5   The dipyridamole treatment was stopped on 8 August.

TRUE/FALSE

6   The patient should be given 40 mg of simvastatin in the evening.

TRUE/FALSE

7   You can only find 80 mg simvastatin tablets in stock, scored down the middle. You can split one tablet in half to give the correct daily dose.

TRUE/FALSE

8   A 20 mg injection of furosemide is required every morning.

TRUE/FALSE

9   The patient has been prescribed budesonide 200 microgram twice daily.

TRUE/FALSE

10   Budesonide was not available on the ward until 2 August.

TRUE/FALSE

11 Budesonide is a powder supplied in capsules. By midday of 7 August the patient had swallowed a total of 11 capsules.

TRUE/FALSE

12 Each capsule of budesonide contains 0.02 mg of the drug.

TRUE/FALSE

13 The total amount of budesonide taken this month is 2.4 mg.

TRUE/FALSE

14 The patient takes a single 5 mg dose of propafenone daily.

TRUE/FALSE

15 All of Mr McMahon's drugs have been written up by Dr A Ahmed.

TRUE/FALSE

MEDICATION ADMINISTRATION RECORD – sample E (1 of 2)
PATIENT'S NAME: JAMES McMAHON

ROUTE	*p.o.*	MEDICINE						DR's SIGNATURE					
DATE	1/8	*Lanzoprazole*						*A Ahmed*					
	DOSE	1	2	3	4	5	6	7	8	9	10	11	12
Morning	**15 mg**	KS	4	BI	KS	CR	CR	KS					
Midday													
Evening													
Bedtime													

ROUTE	*p.o.*	MEDICINE						DR's SIGNATURE					
DATE	1/8	*Dipyridamole*						*A Ahmed*					
	DOSE	1	2	3	4	5	6	7	8	9	10	11	12
Morning	**200 mg**	KS	KS	BI	KS	4	4	4					
Midday													
Evening	**200 mg**	KS	KS	BI	KS	4	4	4					
Bedtime													

ROUTE	*p.o.*	MEDICINE						DR's SIGNATURE					
DATE	1/8	*Simvastatin*						*A Ahmed*					
	DOSE	1	2	3	4	5	6	7	8	9	10	11	12
Morning													
Midday													
Evening													
Bedtime	**40 mg**	TD	TD	TD	CJ	CJ	CJ	KS					

Non administration codes: 4 = refused; 5 = medication unavailable

MEDICATION ADMINISTRATION RECORD – sample E (2 of 2)
PATIENT'S NAME: JAMES McMAHON

ROUTE	*p.o.*	MEDICINE						DR's SIGNATURE					
DATE	1/8	*Furosemide*						*A Ahmed*					
	DOSE	1	2	3	4	5	6	7	8	9	10	11	12
Morning	20 mg	KS	4	BI	KS	CR	CR	KS					
Midday													
Evening													
Bedtime													

ROUTE	*inh*	MEDICINE						DR's SIGNATURE					
DATE	1/8	*Budesonide*						*A Ahmed*					
	DOSE	1	2	3	4	5	6	7	8	9	10	11	12
Morning	200 μg	5	KS	BI	KS	CR	CR	KS					
Midday													
Evening	200 μg	5	KS	BI	KS	CR	CR	KS					
Bedtime													

ROUTE	*p.o.*	MEDICINE						DR's SIGNATURE					
DATE	1/8	*Prednisolone*						*J Hussain*					
	DOSE	1	2	3	4	5	6	7	8	9	10	11	12
Morning	5 mg	KS	KS	BI	KS	CR	CR	KS					
Midday													
Evening													
Bedtime													

Non administration codes: 4 = refused; 5 = medication unavailable

Test 57

Using sample treatment sheet F, decide whether the statements written below are true or false. You will need to examine each of the four statements carefully to spot the errors. Two statements are false and two are true.

1 The patient takes 70 mg of alendronic acid (Fosamax®) once weekly in the morning before breakfast.

TRUE/FALSE

2 The patient should be wearing a 25 microgram/hour fentanyl patch (Durogesic®) which is to be renewed every 48 hours.

TRUE/FALSE

3 On the morning of the 14th, blood should be taken to check the vancomycin levels.

TRUE/FALSE

4 The patient takes 24 units of Actrapid® insulin per day split into morning and evening doses.

TRUE/FALSE

MEDICATION ADMINISTRATION RECORD – SAMPLE F

ROUTE	*p.o.*	MEDICINE					DR's SIGNATURE					
DATE	11/10	*Alendronic acid*					*A Ahmed*					
	DOSE	11	12	13	14	15	16	17	18	19	20	21	22
0630	70 mg	X	X	X	TD	X	X	X	X	X	X		X
1200													

ROUTE	*p.o.*	MEDICINE					DR's SIGNATURE					
DATE	11/10	*Fentanyl Patch*					*A Ahmed*					
	DOSE	11	12	13	14	15	16	17	18	19	20	21	22
0800	25 micrograms	TD	X	X		X	X		X	X		X	X
1200													

ROUTE	*i.v.*	MEDICINE					DR's SIGNATURE					
DATE	11/10	*Vancomycin*					*A Ahmed*					
	DOSE	11	12	13	14	15	16	17	18	19	20	21	22
0800													
1200	750 mg	TD	KS	CR									
1700				check									

ROUTE	*s.c.*	MEDICINE					DR's SIGNATURE					
DATE	11/10	*Actrapid insulin*					*A Ahmed*					
	DOSE	11	12	13	14	15	16	17	18	19	20	21	22
0800	4 Units	TD	KS	CR									
1200													
1700	2U nits	TD	KS	CR									
2100													

CHAPTER 6

Mock tests

Introduction to the tests

This final section contains an entrance-type numerical test of 30 questions followed by three nursing calculation mock tests of 50 questions each. Each test comes with expanded answers (page 159). The numerical test is multiple choice: choose from answer A, B, C or D and circle it. To complete the three mock tests you will first have to decide what type of question is being asked and what calculations are necessary. There are four basic types of calculation, which are:

1 Unit conversion (metric units).
2 Drug dosage ('number of measures').
3 Concentrations (strength of dose).
4 Rates (dose per time).

1 Make sure you are familiar with the metric system of measurement, especially metric weights and volumes and their abbreviations.
Maths required: multiplication and division by powers of 10 (especially by 1000) and the positioning of the decimal point.

2 When calculating the number of measures (tablets, spoonfuls, ampoules etc) make sure that the dose prescribed and the dose per measure are in the same metric units. If the question asks for the *volume*, you need to *multiply the number of measures by the volume of one measure*.
Maths required: division, multiplication and cancelling of fractions and whole numbers.

3 Concentrations can be used to work out the *quantity* of drug in a given volume of solution.
Maths required: multiplication of whole numbers and decimals.

4 *Rate* questions always include the *time period*. Expect to have to work out either the length of time needed to administer a prescribed dose, or the total amount of drug infused for a given time period, or the *drop rate*.
Maths required: multiplication and division of whole numbers, fractions and decimals.

Time limits have been set for the tests. The numerical test should be easy to complete in the allotted time. The three mock tests are more difficult. Only the best candidates will be able to complete all of the questions in the hour allowed. If you get stuck on a question, *you must leave it* and move on to the next question. Aim to pick up as many marks as you can as quickly as possible by answering the easier questions first. These are usually the shorter questions or 'one liners'. You get one mark for answering an easy question correctly and one mark for answering a difficult question correctly. Your goal is to achieve 40 correct answers out of 50 questions.

No special knowledge of drugs is required to answer the tests. Calculators should not be used to answer any of the questions.

Nursing numerical test

Time allowed: 30 minutes
NO CALCULATORS
Choose answer A, B, C or D and circle it.
Pass mark = 25 correct answers out of 30 questions.

1 How many hours are there between 07:00 hours and 16:30 hours?

A. 7.5 hours   B. 8.5 hours   C. 9.5 hours   D. 10.5 hours

2 What is 400 mg in grams?

A. 0.25 g   B. 0.4 g   C. 0.25 g   D. 0.04 g

3 A nursing test contains 40 questions. You answer 32 questions correctly. What is this in percent?

A. 70%   B. 75%   C. 80%   D. 90%

4 What is 2200 ml in litres?

A. 22 L   B. 2 L   C. 0.2 L   D. 2.2 L

5 If 15 is divided by 9 what is the answer to three decimal places?

A. 0.67   B. 1.67   C. 1.666   D. 1.667

6 What is 25.4 ÷ 0.04?

A. 635   B. 101.6   C. 63.5   D. 10.16

7 How many micrograms are there in 0.05 milligrams?

A. 0.5   B. 5   C. 50   D. 500

8 One 0.1 ml drop of water drips from a tap every three seconds. How much water is wasted per hour?

A. 12 ml   B. 120 ml   C. 1.2 L   D. 12 L

9 What is 200 milligrams as a fraction of 1 gram?

A. $\frac{1}{4}$ B. $\frac{1}{5}$ C. $\frac{1}{2}$ D. $\frac{2}{5}$

10 You have £4.50 and then spend 85 pence. How much money have you got left?

A. £3.55   B. £3.45   C. £3.75   D. £3.65

11 What is the weight in kg when 10 g is added to 1 kg?

A. 1.001 kg   B. 1.10 kg   C. 1.01 kg   D. 10.1 kg

12 A 500 ml bottle is three-quarters full of liquid. How much liquid does it contain?

A. 375 ml   B. 360 ml   C. 400 ml   D. 350 ml

13 There are eight men and 42 women in a class of nursing students. What percentage are men?

A. 16%   B. 24%   C. 10%   D. 12%

14 $25 \div \frac{5}{6} =$

A. 15   B. 20   C. 25   D. 30

15 $\frac{5}{8}$ as a decimal is:

A. 0.625   B. 0.675   C. 0.725   D. 0.75

16 $4(4 \times 3 - 2) =$

A. 46   B. 40   C. 14   D. 16

17 $3\frac{3}{16} \times 1\frac{1}{3} =$

A. 4.25   B. 4.5   C. 5   D. 5.25

18 60% as a fraction is:

A. $\frac{5}{6}$ B. $\frac{3}{5}$ C. $\frac{2}{3}$ D. $\frac{7}{10}$

19 If your shift started at 07:30 hours and finished at 17:00 hours, how many hours were you on duty if you took a 30-minute lunch break?

A. 9 hours   B. 8.5 hours   C. 8.0 hours   D. 7.5 hours

20 Dividing 20 by 0.004 gives:

A. 50   B. 500   C. 5000   D. 50 000

21 Expressed as a decimal 22% is:

A. 0.11   B. 0.22   C. 2.2   D. 0.2

22 If 1.8 gram of a drug is divided into four equal doses, how much is one dose?

A. 350 mg   B. 375 mg   C. 450 mg   D. 475 mg

23 A 7 mg dose of a drug is prescribed. Tablets come in sizes of 1, 3, and 5 mg. What is the least number of tablets you can administer?

A. 7   B. 5   C. 4   D. 3

24 A patient takes 500 mg of a drug every six hours. How many grams is this per day?

A. 2 g   B. 3 g   C. 4 g   D. 5 g

25 A pump delivers 125 ml of fluid per hour. How long will it take to deliver one litre?

A. 9 hours   B. 8 hours   C. 7 hours   D. 6 hours

26 30 mg ÷ 12 =

A. 2.4 mg   B. 2.5 mg   C. 4 mg   D. 0.25 mg

27 If a man weighing 90 kg loses 10% of his weight in hospital, what is his new weight?

A. 78 kg   B. 79 kg   C. 80 kg   D. 81 kg

28 Which of the fractions is the same size as five-sixths?

A. $\frac{16}{24}$ B. $\frac{14}{18}$ C. $\frac{25}{30}$ D. $\frac{9}{12}$

29 What is 4% of 2 litres?

A. 8 ml   B. 10 ml   C. 40 ml   D. 80 ml

30 1 gram – 25 milligrams =

A. 0.975 g   B. 907.5 mg   C. 990.75 mg   D. 1.975 mg

Guide to the mock tests

The following abbreviations are used in these mock tests.

g = grams
mg = milligrams
L = litres
ml = millilitres
% = per cent
/ = per; as in mg/hour (milligrams per hour)
p.o. = orally
s/c = subcutaneous
prn = when required
stat = at once
o.d. = once daily
b.d. = twice daily
t.d.s. = three times daily
q.d.s. = four times daily
1/52 = for one week
TDD, tdd = total daily dose
dp = decimal place

Nursing calculation mock test 1

Time allowed: one hour.

NO CALCULATORS

Pass mark = 40 correct answers out of 50 questions.

1   The patient takes 700 mg of allopurinol daily, divided into three doses. 200 mg is given at midday and again in the evening. What dose is given in the morning?

2   Convert 0.025 milligrams to micrograms.

3   The patient inhales 1.2 mg of budesonide powder daily. How many 200 microgram capsules is this?

4   Metformin is prescribed; 500 mg with breakfast for 10 days, followed by 500 mg with breakfast and evening meal for the next 10 days, then 500 mg with breakfast, lunch and evening meal for the next 10 days. How many grams of metformin has the patient taken in total in 30 days?

5   40 mg of gliclazide is prescribed. Stock is 80 mg tablets scored. What do you give?

6   The prescription asks for carbamazepine (Tegretol®) 600 mg b.d. How many grams of Tegretol® does the patient take daily?

7   The patient is prescribed dexamethasone 2 mg/6 hours p.o. for 2 days. What is the total amount of dexamethasone taken over this period?

8   The patient needs 150 mg of amitriptyline. The stock is an oral solution containing 50 mg in 5 ml. What volume do you measure out?

9   An oral solution of verapamil contains 40 mg of the drug in 5 ml of solution. What is the concentration in mg/ml?

10 How many grams of dextrose are there in 20 ml of 5% w/v dextrose infusion fluid?

11 Change 200 micrograms/minute to mg/hour.

12 The treatment is 1 sachet of Klaricid® b.d. for 7 days. If each sachet contains 250 mg of clarithromycin, how many grams of the drug in total will be consumed over the seven-day period?

13   The patient is written up for paracetamol 1 g q.d.s. If the tablets are 500 mg each, how many do you give per day?

14   500 ml of dextrose 5% is administered at a rate of 100 ml/hour. How long will the infusion last?

15   The prescription reads gentamycin 160 mg stat i/m. You have 40 mg/ml 6 ml ampoules. What volume should you give?

16   An infusion pump is set to deliver 50 ml of infusion fluid per hour. The pump is switched on at 11:00 hrs. How much should it have infused by 1330 hrs?

17   Metoclopramide (Maxolon®) oral solution is to be given. The dose is 10 mg and the stock strength is 5 mg in 5 ml. How much do you give?

18   The patient is given 0.5 millilitres of concentrated oral morphine solution (Oramorph®) 100 mg/5 ml. How many milligrams is this?

19   If 80 mg of pethidine is to be administered i/m and the stock is a 50 mg/ml in 2 ml ampoules, what volume should be drawn up?

20   The patient needs naxalone (Narcan®) by intravenous injection. Stock is a 400 microgram/ml vial. What volume do you draw up for a dose of 150 microgram? Give your answer to the nearest one hundredth of an ml (to two dp).

21   The patient has been prescribed hyoscine hydrobromide (Kwells®) 0.6 mg s/c every 4 hours. How many micrograms are there in one dose?

22   The prescription asks for alfacalcidol (One-Alpha®) oral drops 2 micrograms/ml. If there are 20 drops per ml, how many micrograms are there in one drop?

23   Glycereol suppositories contain 70% w/w glycerol as active ingredient. How much glycerol is contained in one 4 gram suppository?

24   The patient is given 50 ml of 20% w/v glucose intravenous infusion fluid. How many grams of glucose is this?

25   The maximum daily dose of metoclopramide is 500 microgram/kg. How many milligrams of metoclopramide can a patient weighing 75 kg take every 24 hours?

26 Diazepam (Valium®) is diluted for infusion to give a solution containing 80 mg/L. If after 8 hours the patient had received 48 mg of Valium®, what was the infusion rate in ml/hour?

27 An infusion of amiodarone is ordered 0.5 mg/minute for 6 hours. How much amiodarone should be drawn up?

28 You are to administer 600 mg of dipyridamole (Persantin®) per day in 3 divided doses of equal size. You have an oral suspension 50 mg per 5 ml. How much do you give per dose?

29 Heparin is to be given by subcutaneous injection. A 0.2 ml syringe of heparin contains 25 000 units of heparin per ml. How many units are there per syringe?

30 The treatment is an intravenous infusion of flecainide 100 microgram/kg/hour for 12 hours. The patient weighs 60 kg and the stock is 10 mg/ml 15 ml ampoules. What volume of flecainide will need to be drawn up and added to the infusion fluid?

31 The patient has been prescribed 1.5 mg of digoxin to be given in 4 divided doses of equal size, 6 hours apart. How many milligrams are there in one divided dose?

32 A 1.2 g vial of co-amoxiclav (Augmentin®) powder is reconstituted to give 20 ml of solution. How much should be added to the infusion bag for a dose of 1 gram? Give your answer to the nearest tenth of a millilitre (to one dp).

33 The patient self-administers glyceryl trinitrate (GTN) aerosol spray, 400 microgram per metered dose. How many milligrams of GTN are contained in a 200-dose unit?

34 The prescription is disodium etidronate (Didronel®) 5 mg/kg. You have 200 mg tablets and the patient weighs 80 kg. How many tablets are required?

35 A 5 ml ampoule of co-trimoxazole 96 mg/ml is diluted with glucose 5% w/v to give 125 ml of intravenous infusion fluid. If the patient receives a dose of 8 mg/minute, what is the infusion rate in ml/hour?

36 A fentanyl transdermal patch (Durogesic®) has been prescribed. It releases fentanyl through the skin at a rate of 100 microgram/hour for three days. How much fentanyl will have been released after this time?

37   Cefuroxime is prescribed by intravenous infusion (ivi). 1 g of powder is reconstituted with 50 ml of 5% w/v glucose and the solution given over 40 minutes. How many milligrams per minute does the patient receive?

38   What is 1 ml/minute converted to litres/day?

39   Lidocaine (lignocaine) 0.2% is available ready mixed in glucose 5% w/v infusion fluid. If the infusion rate is set at 4 mg/minute, what is the flow rate in ml/hour?

40   The patient is started on 0.9% w/v sodium chloride by subcutaneous infusion using a 20 drops/ml giving set. You check the drop rate and see that it is 14 drops in 30 seconds. Approximately what volume would you expect to see infused after 12 hours?

41   500 mg of amoxicillin is reconstituted with 2.5 ml of water and then diluted with sodium chloride 0.9% w/v infusion fluid to give a volume of 50 ml. What is the concentration in mg/ml?

42   100 ml of metrondiazole (Flagyl®) suspension contains 4 g of the drug. How much do you give for a dose of 800 mg?

43   A patient weighing 80 kg is administered 100 ml of isotonic gentamycin (Viaflex® bag) 800 micrograms/ml over 30 minutes. What is the dose in mg/kg?

44   The treatment is pantoprazole (Protium®) 40 mg by intravenous infusion. Stock is a 40 mg vial of powder reconstituted with sodium chloride 0.9% w/v and diluted to 100 ml. What is the concentration of pantoprazole in the infusion fluid in microgram/ml?

45   The patient is prescribed a seven-day course of aciclovir 800 mg 5 times per day. How many grams of aciclovir in total will be consumed over the seven-day period?

46   1.5 litres of saline is to be given over 10 hours using a 20 drop/ml giving set. What is the drop rate in drops per minute?

47   A syringe driver contains 20 mg of morphine and 150 mg of cyclizine in 6 ml of solution. The entire contents of the syringe are infused in 24 hours. What is the dose rate for the cyclizine in mg/hour?

48 The patient needs 28 units of insulin in the morning and 22 units in the evening, by subcutaneous injection. Stock is a 10 ml vial containing 100 units/ml. How many days supply of insulin are available per vial?

49 How much fluid will a 20 drop/ml giving set deliver over 12 hours if the drop rate is set to 60 drops/minute?

50 Epinephrine (adrenaline) is required. The stock is labelled as '1 in 10 000' (1 g in 10 000 ml) and you need to administer 1 mg. What volume do you give?

Nursing calculation mock test 2

Time allowed: one hour

NO CALCULATORS

Pass mark = 40 correct answers out of 50 questions.

1   The patient is written up for ibuprofen (Brufen®) 1.2 g daily in four divided doses. How much Brufen® is there in one dose?

2   The patient is started on quetiapine (Seroquel®) 25 mg b.d. on day 1, 50 mg b.d. on day 2, 100 mg b.d. on day 3 and 150 mg b.d. on day 4. How many milligrams of drug in total have been administered by the end of the fourth day?

3   Convert 0.0015 gram to milligrams.

4   Erythromycin is to be given 250 mg q.d.s. What is the total daily dose?

5   The prescription asks for carvedilol 3.125 mg b.d. How many microgram are there per dose?

6   Your patient is prescribed digoxin 500 microgram stat p.o. The dose is repeated after 12 hours. How much digoxin has the patient received in total?

7   Phenobarbital elixir is to be given. The dose is 90 mg and the stock strength is 15 mg/5 ml. How much do you give?

8   An intravenous infusion of trimethoprim 200 mg is ordered. Stock is 20 mg/ml in 5 ml ampoules. How many ampoules are required?

9   A 10 ml syringe contains 20 mg of morphine. What is the concentration of morphine in mg/ml?

10 Persantin® (dipyridamole) oral suspension 50 mg/5 ml is prescribed. If the total daily dose is 300 mg, how many days supply is there in a 150 ml bottle?

11 Convert 7.2 mg/day to micrograms per minute.

12 The prescription asks for Serc® (betahistine) 16 mg t.d.s. Stock is 8 mg tablets. How many tablets of Serc® does the patient take each day?

13 An infusion of dobutamine in 1.5 L of glucose 5% w/v commences at 0900 hours. If the flow rate is 120 ml per hour at what time will the infusion finish?

14 An intravenous infusion of aciclovir (Zovirax®) is prescribed. A 500 mg vial of Zovirax® powder is reconstituted with 20 ml of water. How much should be drawn up and added to the infusion bag for a dose of 400 mg?

15 If one litre of saline (0.9% w/v) is to be in infused over 12 hours, how much should have been infused after 30 minutes, to the nearest millilitre?

16 250 ml of colloid (Gelofusine®) is given i.v. stat over 15 minutes. What is the exact flow rate in ml/minute?

17 If an infusion pump delivers 120 ml in 90 minutes, what infusion rate is the pump set to in ml/hour?

18 A patient is to receive 500 mg of flucloxacillin. You have an oral solution of strength 125 mg/5 ml. What volume should you administer?

19 The prescription asks for 20 mg of oral morphine (Oramorph®). Stock vials are 30 mg/5 ml. What volume of Oramorph® is wasted (left in the vial) after drawing up the drug? Give your answer to one dp.

20 Insulin syringes, with needles attached, come in sizes of 1 ml and are graduated in units (U) where 100 U = 1 ml. What is the volume of 35 units?

21 Bactroban® ointment contains 2% w/w mupirocin as active ingredient. How many milligrams of mupirocin are present in a 15 g tube of Bactroban®?

22 Dextrose-saline contains one-fifth as much sodium chloride as 0.9% w/v sodium chloride infusion fluid. What percentage is this?

23 How many grams of glucose will the patient receive if the order states 25 ml of 50% w/v glucose stat i/v.

24 The prescription asks for gentamicin 5 mg/kg daily in divided doses every 8 hours. If the patient weighs 60 kg, how much should be administered in one divided dose?

25 One litre of sodium chloride 0.9% w/v infusion fluid is given at a rate of 60 drops per minute using a 20 drop/ml giving set. How long should the infusion last in hours and minutes to the nearest minute?

26 Amiodarone, 30 mg/ml is available in a 10 ml pre-filled syringe. How much amiodarone does it contain?

27 The prescription calls for dobutamine by intravenous infusion 5 microgram/kg/minute. How many milligrams of dobutamine should have been infused after 10 hours if the patient weighs 72 kg?

28 Your patient has been prescribed the drug quetiapine (Seroquel®) 450 mg in two divided doses. If the first dose is 250 mg, what is the second dose?

29 A 5 mg dose of salbutamol (Ventolin®) is given at a rate of 10 microgram/minute in 5% w/v glucose infusion fluid. How long with the infusion last to the nearest hour?

30 Quinine is given at a rate of 20 microgram/kg/minute. How much quinine is required per day for a patient weighing 50 kg?

31 The patient is written up for an intravenous infusion of mentro-ndiazole (Flagyl®) 500 mg given over 20 minutes, every 8 hours. You have 5 mg/ml 100 ml Viaflex® bags of Flagyl®. How many bags do you need for the first day?

32 How much furosemide (frusemide) solution of strength 4 mg/ml should be administered for a 20 mg dose?

33 Solian® solution (amisulpride) is prescribed. The stock strength is 100 mg/ml. How much is drawn up for a 500 mg dose?

34 The order is metrondiazole (Flagyl®) 400 mg p.o. t.d.s. 1/52. How much Flagyl® will be administered over this period?

35 Atenolol 150 microgram/kg is to be administered to a patient weighing 86 kg. Stock is 500 microgram/ml 10 ml ampoules. What volume do you draw up?

36 An injection of bupivaciane (Marcain®) 0.25% w/v is to be administered. What is the concentration in mg/ml?

48 A syringe driver contains 40 mg of metoclopramide (Maxolon®) and 100 mg of diamorphine (heroin) in 8 ml of solution. The entire contents of the syringe are infused in 24 hours. What is the dose rate for the diamorphine in mg/hour (to one dp)?

49 The patient self-administers 20 units of insulin by subcutaneous injection, twice daily, using a reusable pen injector. How many days will two 3 ml 100 units/ml pen cartridges last?

50 You need to administer lidocaine (lignocaine) at a rate of 1 mg/minute. You have a 500 ml bag of 5% w/v glucose infusion fluid containing 1 gram of lignocaine. What is the infusion rate in ml/hour?

37 If 20 mg of diazepam (Valium®) is infused in 500 m chloride 0.9% w/v infusion fluid what is the concer the drug in microgram/ml?

38 120 mg of diamorphine is to be given by continuo cutaneous infusion every 24 hours. How much diam should the patient have received after four hours?

39 The patient is written up for bumetanide by intrave infusion. Two 500 microgram/ml 4 ml ampoules are d up and diluted with sodium chloride 0.9% w/v to give 500 m infusion fluid. What is the concentration of bumetanide in infusion fluid in mg/L?

40 1 gram of co-amoxiclav (Augmentin®) is to be infused ove 8 hours. You have 600 mg vials of powder for reconstitution. How many vials is this equivalent to (to two dp)?

41 100 ml of reconstituted ciprofloxacin (Ciproxin®) suspension contains 5 g of the drug. How much do you give for a dose of 500 mg?

42 100 ml of metrondiazole (Flagyl®) suspension contains 4 g of the drug. How much do you give for a dose of 500 mg?

43 If a 750 mg vial of cefuroxime powder is reconstituted water to give a solution of volume 7.5 ml, what is the concentration in mg/ml?

44 Cipramil® (citalopram) oral drops are prescribed. A 15 ml bottle contains 600 mg of the drug. How many milligrams of the drug are present in one 0.05 ml drop?

45 600 ml of fluid is to be infused over 4 hours using a 20 drops/ml giving set. Calculate the drops per minute.

46 An elixir of digoxin (Lanoxin-PG®) contains 50 microgram per millilitre. How many 250 microgram doses are there in a 60 ml bottle of Lanoxin-PG®?

47 A vial containing 500 mg of vancomycin powder is re-constituted with 'water for injection' to give 10 ml of solution. What dose is obtained by drawing up 2.5 ml of the vancomycin solution?

Nursing calculation mock test 3

Time allowed: one hour

NO CALCULATORS

Pass mark = 40 correct answers out of 50 questions.

1   The patient is prescribed 1 g amoxicillin per day in four divided doses. Stock is a 250 mg/5 ml oral suspension. How many days supply are there in a 100 ml bottle?

2   Write 0.0625 milligram in micrograms.

3   The treatment is lithium carbonate 0.4–1.2 g daily in two divided doses. What is the maximum number of 200 mg tablets that can be given for one dose?

4   The controlled drugs cupboard contains two bottles of temazepam oral solution 10 mg/5 ml for a patient who takes 20 mg of the drug at bedtime. One bottle contains enough temazepam for 30 doses. What volume of temazepam would you expect to see recorded in the controlled drugs book on receipt of the medication (two full bottles)?

5   A child is to be given sodium valproate (Epilim®) syrup 200 mg/5 ml. The dose is 20 mg/kg daily in two divided doses. Calculate the volume of one dose if the child weighs 16 kg.

6   Ciprofloxacin (Ciproxin®) for infusion is available in 2 mg/ml glass vials. How much ciprofloxacin is there in a 200 ml vial?

7   You have a 3% w/v solution of a drug. The patient requires 60 mg. What volume do you give?

8   How many milligrams of phenytoin (Epanutin®) are there in a 15 ml dose of a 30 mg/5 ml suspension?

9   A patient requires an infusion of dopamine (Intropin®) at a rate of 5 microgram/kg/minute for 12 hours. How many milligrams of dopamine are required if the patient weighs 92 kg?

10   Lidocaine (lignocaine) 2% is to be injected. If the maximum dose is 200 mg what is the maximum volume?

11   A 300 mg bolus dose of amiodarone is given by intravenous injection over 4 minutes. Stock is a 30 mg/ml 10 ml pre-filled syringe. What is the flow rate in ml/minute?

12   An injection of 12 units of Human Mixtard® is ordered. Stock is 100 units/ml 10 ml vial. You draw up 12 units into the insulin syringe. How many ml is this?

13   The patient is written up for an oral suspension of Tegretol® (carbamazepine) 20 ml t.d.s. If the label on the bottle reads 'Tegretol 100 mg/5 ml' what is the daily dose of carbamazepine in grams?

14   One gram of vancomycin is prescribed by intermittent intravenous infusion at a rate not to exceed 10 mg/minute. What is the minimum length of time for this infusion?

15   The patient is prescribed Jevity® liquid to be PEG fed at a rate of 75 ml/hr for 20 hrs. How many 500 ml stock bottles will be required?

16   How many milligrams of lidocaine (lignocaine) are there in 1 ml of 0.5% lidocaine?

17   Ranitidine (Zantac®) in the form of sugar-free syrup has been prescribed for a child. The dose is 2 mg/kg, the stock strength is 75 mg/5 ml and the child weighs 22.5 kg. What volume should be drawn up?

18   How many micrograms of adrenaline are there in 1 ml of 1 in 10 000 adrenaline?

19   A 500 mg vial of vancomycin powder is reconstituted to a volume of 10 ml with sterile water for injection. What volume should be drawn up for a dose of 300 mg?

20   The patient is written up for a 15 mg/kg loading dose of phenytoin with a maintenance dose of 75 mg t.d.s. The stock strength is 50 mg/ml. The patient weighs 60 kg. What volume of phenytoin is required for the first day of treatment?

21   Morphine is to be infused at a rate of 1.25 mg/hr. Stock is a 2 mg/ml 50 ml vial. What volume will be required for a 24-hour infusion?

22   How many grams of sodium chloride are there in a 500 ml pack of 0.9% w/v physiological saline?

23 How many grams of sodium chloride are there in 1 L of 0.18% w/v sodium chloride and 4% glucose solution?

24 If 1 L of 0.9% physiological saline contains 150 mmol (millimoles) of sodium chloride, how many mmol are there in 1 L of 0.18% sodium chloride solution?

25 An injection of enoxaparin (Clexane®) 1.5 mg/kg is to be given. The patient weighs 60 kg. Stock is a 1 ml pre-filled Clexane® 100 mg/ml syringe with graduation marks every 2.5 mg. How many graduations will have to be expelled (wasted) before you can give the injection?

26 A patient-controlled analgesia (PCA) infusion pump contains morphine 1 mg/ml. The patient receives a bolus dose of 1 ml when the button is pressed. If the minimum period between doses ('lock-out time') is set to 6 minutes, what is the maximum dose of morphine available to the patient in mg/hr?

27 The PCA prescription is for fentanyl 25 microgram/ml with a 20 microgram/6 minute lock-out time. What is the volume of each bolus dose?

28 An injection of 10 000 units of heparin is ordered. Stock is a 25 000 units/ml 1 ml ampoule. What volume should be drawn up?

29 The patient is to receive an infusion of heparin 1000 units/ml. You draw up two 5 ml ampoules, four 1 ml ampoules and a further 0.4 ml from a 1 ml ampoule. The heparin is diluted to 24 ml with 0.9% saline and given at a rate of 2 ml/hr via a syringe driver. Calculate the dose rate in units/hour.

30 The patient is prescribed an infusion of heparin, 1000 units/hr. In stock is a 5 ml 5000 units/ml ampoule which is diluted to 50 ml with 0.9% saline. What is the rate of the infusion in ml/hr?

31 The treatment is an intravenous infusion of imipenem with cilastatin (Primaxin®). The total daily dose (TDD) should not exceed 50 mg/kg/day or 4 g/day. What is the TDD for a patient weighing 82 kg?

32 How many milligrams of potassium chloride are there in 1 ml of 15% potassium chloride solution?

33   What is the difference in milligrams per day between 5 mg t.d.s. and 5 mg tdd?

34   How many grams of paracetamol are there in 10 ml of paediatric oral suspension (Calpol®) 120 mg/5 ml?

35   The treatment is 3.054 g lithium citrate oral solution (Li-liquid®) daily in two divided doses. Stock is an oral solution containing 509 mg/5 ml. What volume do you measure out for one dose?

36   A patient is to receive an intravenous infusion of aminophylline at a rate of 36 mg/hour. Stock is a 25 mg/ml 10 ml ampoule of aminophylline mixed with glucose 5% w/v to give 500 ml of intravenous infusion fluid. What is the infusion rate in ml/hour?

37   A one litre bottle of Jevity® liquid is fed via a pump. The rate is set to 100 ml/hr and the pump is switched on at 2200 hours. The rate is increased at 0200 hours. If the feed finished at 0700 hours what was the rate increased to?

38   A child is to receive an infusion of insulin at a rate of 0.1 units/kg/hour. The syringe pump contains 50 units of insulin in 50 ml of 0.9 % sodium chloride. At what speed in ml/hour should the pump be set at for a child weighing 40 kg?

39   Convert 1 microgram/minute to mg/day.

40   500 ml of sodium chloride 0.9% w/v is to be given subcutaneously over 10 hours using a 20 drop/ml giving set. What is the drop rate in drops per minute to the nearest drop?

41   What is a 0.05% w/v solution in micrograms/ml?

42   The prescription is for a sugar-free oral solution of furosemide (Frusol®). What is the concentration of the stock in mg/ml if a 5 ml dose contains 40 mg of the drug?

43   The daily therapeutic dose of ceftriaxone (Rocephin®) for infants and children of up to 12 years is 20–50 mg/kg body weight. What is the maximum daily dose for a 10-year-old child weighing 38 kg?

44   The weight of a child up to age 10 years can be estimated from the equation: weight in kg $= 2 \times$ (age $+$ 4). Estimate the weight of a seven-year-old child?

45   The treatment is 20 mg of omeprazole (Losec®) o.d. for 8 weeks. How many grams of omeprazole will be consumed in total?

46   A 1 g vial of cefotaxime powder is reconstituted with 4.2 ml of water for injection. If the volume of the solution is 5 ml how much water has the powder displaced?

47   A 250 mg vial of flucloxacillin powder is reconstituted with 9.7 ml of water for injection. The displacement volume is 0.3 ml. What volume do you draw up for a dose of 250 mg?

48   A 500 mg vial of vancomycin powder is reconstituted with 9.5 ml of water for injection. The displacement volume is 0.5 ml. What volume do you draw up for a dose of 300 mg?

49   A 750 mg vial of cefuroxime powder is reconstituted with 5.5 ml of water for injection. If the displacement volume is 0.5 ml what volume do you draw up for a dose of 600 mg?

50   A patient weighing 80 kg is written up for a continuous intravenous infusion of dopamine at a rate of 10 microgram/kg/minute. Two 10 ml 40 mg/ml vials of dopamine are diluted to 500 ml with 0.9% sodium chloride. What rate should the infusion pump be set to in ml/hr?

Answers to tests

Basic maths self-assessment test

Remedial level

1　Twenty-five.
2　Four thousand and sixty.
3　Nine hundred and eighty thousand one hundred and seven.
4　3030
5　1 210 000
6　12 500
7　0.3
8　two hundreds; 200.
9　75 pence.
10　11.30 pm.

Level 1

11	20	**16**	15
12	1020	**17**	£3.77
13	136	**18**	5 degrees
14	288	**19**	23 400
15	63	**20**	£11 250

Level 2

21	$7\frac{3}{4}$	**26**	£1020
22	3	**27**	$\frac{1}{5}$
23	15.65	**28**	0.45
24	27	**29**	250 mg
25	76	**30**	1.46

Answers to Chapter 1 test exercises

Test 1

1	1168	**5**	433
2	9042	**6**	18 050
3	2009	**7**	1127
4	27 550	**8**	1112

Test 2

1	63	**6**	95
2	96	**7**	99
3	120	**8**	300
4	92	**9**	1000
5	450	**10**	132

Test 3

1	806	6	10 000
2	2528	7	5511
3	1200	8	5082
4	5080	9	39 975
5	425	10	702

Test 4

1	4	5	410
2	62	6	59
3	113	7	244
4	53	8	125

Test 5

1	30	6	6
2	31	7	38
3	44	8	67
4	45	9	61
5	20	10	206

Test 6

1	14	7	9
2	13	8	56
3	10	9	10
4	2	10	6
5	14	11	6
6	9	12	14

Test 7

1	24	7	39
2	2	8	81
3	5	9	3
4	44	10	36
5	10	11	5
6	21	12	9000

Test 8

1   1 2 3 6
2   1 2 5 10
3   1 2 3 4 8 16 32
4   1 2 3 5 6 9 10 15 18 30 45 90
5   1 2 4 5 10 20 25 50 100 125 250 500
6   8
7   15
8   4
9   50
10   25

Test 9

1	2×3	5	$3\times3\times3\times3$
2	$2\times3\times5$	6	$2\times2\times2\times3\times3\times3$
3	$3\times3\times7$	7	$5\times5\times5$
4	$2\times2\times3\times5\times7$	8	$7\times7\times7$

Test 10

1	2 4 6 8	6	6
2	12 24 36 48	7	60
3	20 40 60 80	8	72
4	25 50 75 100	9	150
5	100 200 300 400	10	200

Answers to Chapter 1 questions

1	2022	16	16
2	610	17	54
3	195	18	80
4	2592	19	26
5	108	20	150
6	64	21	1 2 4 5 10 20
7	5625	22	2 and 5
8	148 473	23	1 2 3 6 7 14 21 42
9	11	24	2, 3 and 7
10	39	25	6 12 18 24 30 36
11	224	26	9 18 27 36 45 54
12	72	27	18
13	130	28	100
14	20	29	250
15	100	30	60

Answers to Chapter 2 test exercises

Test 11

1	$\frac{1}{2}$	6	$\frac{3}{5}$
2	$\frac{3}{4}$	7	$\frac{1}{10}$
3	$\frac{1}{3}$	8	$\frac{19}{20}$
4	$\frac{5}{9}$	9	$\frac{2}{3}$
5	$\frac{2}{3}$	10	$\frac{2}{5}$

Test 12

1	$\frac{7}{8}$	5	1
2	$\frac{5}{6}$	6	$\frac{1}{2}$
3	$\frac{3}{10}$	7	$\frac{2}{3}$
4	$\frac{7}{12}$	8	$\frac{2}{5}$

Test 13

1	15	**4**	$\frac{7}{15}$
2	12	**5**	$\frac{11}{12}$
3	16	**6**	$\frac{7}{16}$

Test 14

1	$\frac{3}{4}$	**4**	$\frac{7}{8}$
2	$\frac{2}{3}$	**5**	$\frac{16}{50}$
3	$\frac{2}{5}$	**6**	$\frac{7}{100}$

Test 15

1	$\frac{2}{27}$	**6**	$\frac{1}{2}$
2	$\frac{8}{45}$	**7**	$\frac{1}{3}$
3	$\frac{16}{63}$	**8**	$\frac{1}{4}$
4	$\frac{2}{27}$	**9**	$\frac{2}{27}$
5	$\frac{3}{500}$	**10**	$\frac{3}{10}$

Test 16

1	$\frac{2}{3}$	**6**	$\frac{2}{5}$
2	$\frac{3}{5}$	**7**	$\frac{1}{25}$
3	$\frac{3}{4}$	**8**	$\frac{1}{50}$
4	$\frac{1}{2}$	**9**	$\frac{1}{20}$
5	$\frac{5}{6}$	**10**	$\frac{2}{3}$

Test 17

1	$\frac{25}{12}$	**5**	$\frac{49}{10}$
2	$\frac{1}{6}$	**6**	$\frac{8}{3}$
3	$\frac{15}{8}$	**7**	$\frac{20}{9}$
4	$\frac{1}{2}$	**8**	50

Test 18

1 $\frac{7}{4}$
2 $\frac{11}{2}$
3 $\frac{17}{6}$
4 $\frac{27}{8}$
5 $\frac{67}{10}$

6 $\frac{119}{100}$
7 $\frac{6}{5}$
8 $\frac{12}{5}$
9 $\frac{7}{5}$

Test 19

1 $4\frac{1}{2}$
2 $5\frac{3}{4}$
3 $5\frac{1}{3}$

4 $16\frac{2}{3}$
5 $5\frac{1}{4}$
6 $12\frac{1}{2}$

Test 20

1 $2\frac{1}{2}$
2 $4\frac{1}{2}$
3 $3\frac{1}{2}$
4 $10\frac{4}{5}$

5 $7\frac{1}{2}$
6 $\frac{3}{20}$
7 $\frac{1}{36}$
8 $\frac{1}{24}$

Test 21

1 $1\frac{2}{5}$
2 $4\frac{1}{4}$
3 8
4 30
5 64
6 72
7 $\frac{5}{8}$
8 $\frac{1}{4}$

9 $\frac{9}{20}$
10 $\frac{1}{2}$
11 $\frac{1}{4}$
12 $\frac{1}{12}$
13 $\frac{1}{5}$
14 $3\frac{3}{5}$
15 $\frac{1}{400}$

Test 22

1 3
2 14
3 8
4 8
5 8

6 5
7 3
8 1
9 5

Test 23

1	22.5	6	a, c, b, d
2	0.275	7	a, d, c, b
3	0.02	8	b, c, a, d
4	200.075	9	a, c, b, d
5	d, b, c, a		

Test 24

1	1589.7	5	17 170.3
2	769.2105	6	25
3	3172.9	7	5.8
4	0.0175	8	100

Test 25

1	8.96	6	160
2	20.02	7	3
3	0.3553	8	100.2
4	0.005 44	9	2032
5	1.5015	10	14 000

Test 26

1	1.7	7	6
2	12.45	8	60
3	8.031 25	9	1.2
4	170	10	62 500
5	33.3	11	20 000
6	11.1	12	0.016

Test 27

1	6.08	3	0.8
2	0.385 43	4	7.96

Test 28

1	4.17	6	160
2	14.2857	7	66
3	10.4	8	17
4	44	9	3
5	81	10	133

Test 29

1	$\frac{3}{5}$	6	$\frac{2}{25}$
2	$\frac{3}{4}$	7	$\frac{19}{20}$
3	$\frac{5}{8}$	8	$1\frac{3}{4}$
4	$\frac{9}{10}$	9	$2\frac{3}{8}$
5	$\frac{1}{1000}$		

Test 30

1	0.3	6	0.875
2	0.25	7	0.85
3	0.4	8	0.105
4	1.25	9	0.18
5	0.12		

Test 31

1	$\frac{1}{5}$ and 0.2	6	$\frac{9}{20}$ and 0.45
2	$\frac{1}{4}$ and 0.25	7	$\frac{7}{20}$ and 0.35
3	$\frac{1}{10}$ and 0.1	8	$\frac{11}{50}$ and 0.22
4	$\frac{3}{4}$ and 0.75	9	$\frac{1}{50}$ and 0.02
5	$\frac{9}{10}$ and 0.9		

Test 32

1	90	4	25
2	60	5	10%
3	125	6	9000

Test 33

1	50%	6	1.5%
2	75%	7	105%
3	100%	8	0.5%
4	20%	9	36%
5	12.5%	10	85%

Answers to Chapter 2 questions

1	$\frac{3}{5}$	11	0.625, $\frac{3}{4}$, 0.905, 0.95, 1.2
2	$\frac{2}{9}$	12	2.2
3	$\frac{3}{8}$	13	5
4	$\frac{2}{7}$	14	0.72
5	$\frac{1}{32}$	15	0.0625
6	$\frac{7}{20}$	16	5000
7	$3\frac{6}{7}$	17	8.38
8	$\frac{9}{2}$	18	0.167
9	$6\frac{1}{8}$	19	$\frac{1}{16}$
10	$\frac{1}{20}$	20	12.5

Answers to Chapter 3 test exercises

Test 34

1	25 micrograms	4	1.275 g
2	1 g	5	0.42 mg
3	330 micrograms		

Test 35

1	1 g	7	325 micrograms
2	2.5 g	8	10 mg
3	1.25 g	9	1.2 kg
4	4.5 mg	10	50 mg
5	500 mg	11	500 micrograms
6	250 mg	12	12 micrograms

Test 36

1	500 ml	6	4.05 L
2	50 ml	7	0.005 L
3	1250 ml	8	0.25 L
4	125 ml	9	0.0105 L
5	2 L	10	10 ml

Test 37

1	kg	6	g
2	L	7	mcg
3	mg	8	g
4	mcg or mg	9	L
5	kg		

Test 38

1	2.1 g	5	0.9 mg
2	1.65 g	6	435 mg
3	3 g	7	0.6005 g
4	0.7 g	8	675 micrograms

Test 39

1	1 g	6	5 mg
2	1.5 g	7	200 micrograms
3	12.5 mg	8	7.5 micrograms
4	2 mg	9	0.5 micrograms
5	0.3 kg	10	2.5 g

Test 40

1	0625 hrs	7	1 hr 33 min
2	1705 hrs	8	18 mins
3	9.50 pm	9	132 secs
4	10.10 am	10	$\frac{2}{3}$
5	7.30 pm	11	54 secs
6	0155 hrs	12	20 secs

Test 41

1	5.5 ml	4	2.5 ml
2	1.5 ml	5	0.55 ml
3	1.2 ml	6	2.8 ml

Test 42

1	0.6 ml	4	0.65 ml
2	1.5 ml	5	1.4 ml
3	0.7 ml	6	0.95 ml

Answers to Chapter 3 questions

1	2 g	11	150 mg
2	400 mg	12	1.1 L
3	250 micrograms	13	1.025 L
4	10 micrograms	14	62 ml
5	80 mg	15	577.5 ml
6	7.5 ml	16	23:30 hrs
7	5.5 g	17	08:30 hrs
8	0.95 ml	18	13:15 hrs
9	7.654 32 g	19	0.05 ml
10	20 mg	20	4 ml

Answers to Chapter 4 test exercises

Test 43

1	3 tablets	**5**	4 ml
2	2 tablets	**6**	3 tablets
3	a) 3 spoonfuls	**7**	4 tablets
	b) 15 ml	**8**	2 spoonfuls
4	a) 2 spoonfuls	**9**	400 mg
	b) 10 ml	**10**	1.25 mg

Test 44

1	a) 0.5 ml	**3**	a) 5 ml
	b) 0.75 ml		b) 2 ml
	c) 1 ml		c) 2.5 ml
	d) 1.5 ml		d) 1 ml
2	a) 3 ml	**4**	a) 20 ml
	b) 2 ml		b) 15 ml
	c) 1 ml		c) 1 ml
	d) 0.4 ml		d) 5 ml

Test 45

1	a) 100	**2**	a) 67 dpm
	b) 80		b) 83 dpm
	c) 16		c) 28 dpm
	d) 30		d) 42 dpm

Test 46

1	20 mg/ml	**7**	20 g
2	10 mg/ml	**8**	1.875 g
3	2.5 mg/ml	**9**	750 units
4	40 mg/ml	**10**	a) 50 mg/ml
5	50 mg/ml		b) 2 mg/ml
6	25 g		

Test 47 with explanations

1 a) 1.6 mg/ml
    b) 267 mcg/min
    c) 0.267 mg/ml
    d) 16.0 mg/hr
    e) 10 ml/hr
    a) 400 mg in 250 ml $= \frac{400}{250} = \frac{40}{25} = \frac{8}{5} = 1\frac{3}{8} = 1.6$ mg/ml
    b) Rate $= 3$ mcg/kg/min $\times 89$ kg $= 267$ mcg/min
    c) 267 mcg/min $= 0.267$ mg/min
    d) 0.267 mg/min $\times 60$ min $= 2.67 \times 6 = 16.02 = 16.0$ mg/hr
       to one decimal place
    e) 16 mg/hr $\div 1.6$ mg/ml in a) $= 160 \div 16 = 10$ ml/hr
       If you find e) difficult, take a one-hour period, then e) becomes
       16 mg $\div 1.6$ mg/ml in 1 hour; 1.6 mg/ml means 1.6 mg in
       1 ml or 16 mg in 10 ml; 10 ml in one hour $= 10$ ml/hr

2 a) 75 mg
    b) 3000 mcg/hr
    c) 3 mg/hr
    d) 0.15 mg/ml
    e) 20 ml/hr
    f) 25 hours
    a) One 3 ml ampoule $= 3$ ml $\times 25$ mg/ml $= 75$ mg
    b) Rate $= 40$ mcg/kg/min $\times 75$ kg $= 3000$ mcg/min
    c) 3000 mcg/hr $= 3$ mg/hr
    d) 75 mg/500 ml $= \frac{75}{500} = \frac{15}{100} = 0.15$ mg/ml
    e) 3 mg/hr $\div 0.15$ mg/ml $= 300 \div 15 = 20$ ml/hr
    f) 500 ml at 20 ml/hr $= \frac{500}{20} = 25$ hours

3 a) 102 ml
    b) 68 dpm
    a) Dose prescribed $= 80$ mg; dose per measure $= 40$ mg
       $\frac{80}{40} \times 1$ ml $= 2$ ml; 100 ml bag $+ 2$ ml drug $= 102$ ml
    b) $102 \div 30 = 3.4$ ml; multiply by 20 drops/min $= 68$ dpm

4   120 ml/hr
Stock is 0.2% w/v = 0.2 g/100 ml = 200 mg/100 ml = 2 mg/ml
Rate = 4 mg/min ÷ 2 mg/ml = 2 ml/min or 120 ml/hr

5   a) 500 mg
b) 10 ml
c) 4 amps
d) 260 ml
e) 130 ml/hr
a) 5 mg/kg × 100 kg = 500 mg
b) Dose prescribed = 500 mg; dose per measure = 50 mg
$\frac{500}{50} \times 1$ ml = 10 ml
c) 10 ml ÷ 3 ml/ampoule = $3\frac{1}{3}$ ampoules; round up to 4 amp
d) Total volume = 250 ml diluent + 10 ml drug = 260 ml
e) Rate in ml/hr = 260 ml/2 hr = 130 ml/hr

6   a) 27 mg
b) 2.7 ml
a) 1.5 mcg/kg × 100 kg × 60 min/hr × 3 hr = 150 × 180 = 27 000 mcg = 27 mg
b) Stock is a 10 mg/ml. Dose prescribed = 27 mg; dose per measure = 10 mg. $\frac{27}{10} \times 1$ ml = 2.7 ml

7   a) 4.25 g
b) 2.125 vials
c) 521.25 ml
d) 2.2 ml/min
a) Dose prescribed = 50 mg/kg × 85 kg = 4250 mg = 4.25 g
b) Each ampoule contains 200 mg/ml × 10 ml = 2000 mg = 2 g. Exact number of vials required = 4.25 ÷ 2 = 2.125 vials
c) Volume = 500 ml + 2.125 vials × 10 ml/vial = 521.25 ml
d) Infusion time = 4 hr × 60 min/hr = 240 mins; infusion rate 521.25 ml ÷ 240 mins = 2.2 ml/min to one decimal point

8   100 hrs
5 mcg/kg/min = 5 × 83 × 60 = 24 900 mcg/hr = 24.9 mg/hr.
Stock = 20 ml × 125 mg/ml = 2500 mg; at 24.9 mg/hr = 100 hrs

Test 48

1   2230 hours
2   250 ml/hr

Test 49

1   mcg/kg/min
       a)   1
       b)   0.5
       c)   2.5
       d)   12.5

Answers to Chapter 4 questions

1	4 tablets	11	2.5 mg/hr
2	2 ml	12	370 mg/hr
3	3 vials	13	8.2 ml
4	10 ml	14	25 ml/hr
5	15 ml	15	0.1 g (100 mg)
6	2.5 ml	16	56 drops/min
7	18 ml	17	50 mg/ml
8	15 ml	18	10 mg/ml
9	4 minutes	19	250 ml
10	80 ml/hr	20	3 mg/ml

Test 50

1	4 tablets	7	3 g
2	400 mg	8	20 mg
3	7.5 g	9	6 amps
4	4 g	10	4 packs
5	none	11	40 tablets
6	12 days	12	30 mg

14   False – the correct drug is prednisolone; be careful with untidy handwriting

15   False – Dr Hussain prescribed the prednisolone

Test 57

1   True (given on the 14th; due again on the 21st)

2   False – a new patch is required every third day (72 hours)

3   True (the doctor has drawn a box on the chart to indicate that a review of the treatment is required; bloods to be taken and vancomycin levels checked)

4   False – the answer is 6 units, split into 4 units in the morning and 2 units in the evening. Be careful with untidy handwriting when a U looks like a zero.

Answers to the nursing numerical test

See also the expanded answers below.

1	C	**16**	B
2	B	**17**	A
3	C	**18**	B
4	D	**19**	A
5	D	**20**	C
6	A	**21**	B
7	C	**22**	C
8	B	**23**	D
9	B	**24**	A
10	D	**25**	B
11	C	**26**	B
12	A	**27**	D
13	A	**28**	C
14	D	**29**	D
15	A	**30**	A

Expanded answers for the nursing numerical test

1 1630 hrs – 0700 hrs = 0930 = 9.5 hrs (C).

2 400 mg ÷ 1000 mg/g = 0.4 g (B).

3 $\frac{32}{40} \times 100\% = \frac{32}{4} \times 10 = 8 \times 10 = 80\%$ (C).

4 2200 ml ÷ 1000 ml/L = 2.2 L (D).

5 $\frac{15}{9} = \frac{5}{3} = 1\frac{2}{3} = 1.6666 = 1.667$ to three decimal points (D).

6 25.4 ÷ 0.04 = 2540 ÷ 4 = 635 (A).

7 0.05 mg × 1000 mcg/mg = 50 micrograms (C).

8 1 drop every 3 seconds and 60 seconds in every minute = 60 ÷ 3 drops per minute = 20 dpm. Each drop = 0.1 ml = 20 × 0.1 ml/min = 2 ml/min = 2 × 60 ml/hr = 120 ml/hr (B).

9 1 gram = 1000 milligrams. 200 mg as a fraction of 1 g is $\frac{200}{1000} = \frac{2}{10} = \frac{1}{5}$ (B).

10 In pence: 450 p – 85 p = 365 p = £3.65 (D).

11 Convert 10 g to kg then add it to 1 kg:
10 g = $\frac{10}{1000}$ kg = 0.01 kg; 1 kg + 0.01 kg = 1.01 kg (C).

12 $500 \times \frac{3}{4} = 125 \times 3 = 375$ ml (A).

13 Total students = 42 + 8 = 50. 8 men: $\frac{8}{50} \times 100\% = 8 \times 2 = 16\%$ men (A).

14 $25 \div \frac{5}{6} = 25 \times \frac{6}{5} = 5 \times 6 = 30$ (D).

15 $8 = 0.\ 6\ 2\ 5$ (A)
$8\overline{)5.5^50^20^40}$

16 Work out the brackets first: 4(4 × 3 – 2) = 4(12 – 2) = 4(10) = 4 × 10 = 40 (B).

17 $3\frac{3}{16} \times 1\frac{1}{3} = \frac{48+3}{16} \times \frac{4}{3} = \frac{51}{16} \times \frac{4}{3} = \frac{17}{4} = 4\frac{1}{4} = 4.25$ (A).

18 60% as a fraction = $\frac{60}{100} = \frac{6}{10} = \frac{3}{5}$ (B).

19 1700 hrs – 0730 hrs = 0930 hrs; less 30 min = 9 hrs (A).

20 20 ÷ 0.004 = 20 000 ÷ 4 = 5000 (C).

21 22% as a decimal = 22 ÷ 100 = 0.22 (B).

22 1.8 g ÷ 4 = 0.45 g × 1000 mg/g = 450 mg (C).

23 7 = 5 + 1 + 1 = 7 mg in 3 tablets (D).

24 Every 6 hours = 4 doses per day. 500 mg × 4 doses/day = 2000 mg/day = 2 g (A).

25 One litre = 1000 ml to be given at a rate of 125 ml/hr. 1000 ml ÷ 125 ml/hr = $\frac{1000}{125}$ hr = 8 hr (B).

26   30 mg ÷ 12 = $\frac{30}{12}$ = $\frac{15}{6}$ = $\frac{5}{2}$ = 2.5 mg (B).

27   90 kg × 10% = 90 × $\frac{10}{100}$ = 9 kg; 90 − 9 = 81 kg (D).

28 $\frac{5}{6}$ = $\frac{10}{12}$ = $\frac{10}{24}$ so not D nor A, which leaves B or C. B = $\frac{14}{18}$ = $\frac{7}{9}$ so not B. C = $\frac{25}{30}$ = $\frac{5}{6}$ (C).

29   4% of 2 L = $\frac{4}{100}$ × 2000 ml = 4 × 20 = 80 ml (D).

30   1 g − 25 mg = 1000 − 25 = 975 mg = 0.975 g (A).

Answers to mock test 1

See also the expanded answers which follow.

1	300 mg	**26**	75 ml/hr
2	25 microgram	**27**	180 mg
3	6 capsules	**28**	20 ml
4	30 g	**29**	5000 units
5	Half a tablet	**30**	7.2 ml
6	1.2 g	**31**	0.375 mg
7	16 mg	**32**	16.7 ml
8	15 ml	**33**	80 mg
9	8 mg/ml	**34**	Two tablets
10	1 g	**35**	125 ml/hr
11	12 mg/hr	**36**	7.2 mg
12	3.5 g	**37**	25 mg/min
13	8 tablets/day	**38**	1.44 L/day
14	5 hours	**39**	120 ml/hr
15	4 ml	**40**	1 L approx
16	125 ml	**41**	10 mg/ml
17	10 ml	**42**	20 ml
18	10 mg	**43**	1 mg/kg
19	1.6 ml	**44**	400 micrograms/ml
20	0.38 ml	**45**	28 g
21	600 micrograms	**46**	50 drops/min
22	0.1 micrograms	**47**	6.25 mg/hr
23	2.8 g	**48**	20 days
24	10 g	**49**	2.16 L
25	37.5 mg	**50**	10 ml

Mock test 1 expanded answers

1 700 mg – 200 mg – 200 mg = *300 mg*.

2 0.025 mg × 1000 mcg/mg = *25 micrograms*.

3 1.2 mg = 1.2 mg × 1000 mcg/mg = 1200 micrograms. 1200 ÷ 200 = *6 capsules*.

4 First 10 days: 500 mg × 10 = 5 g.
Second 10 days: (500 + 500) mg × 10 = 10 g.
Third 10 days: (500 + 500 + 500) mg × 10 = 15 g.
Total = *30 g*.

5 $\frac{40}{80}$ = *half a tablet*.

6 600 mg × 2 = 1200 mg = *1.2 g*.

7 2 mg/dose × 4 doses/day × 2 days = *16 mg*.

8 Dose prescribed = 150 mg; dose per measure = 50 mg. $\frac{150}{50}$ × 5 ml = 3 × 5 ml = *15 ml*.

9 $\frac{40\,mg}{5\,ml}$ = *8 mg/ml*.

10 5% w/v = 5 g/100 ml = 1 g/20 ml. So 20 ml contains *1 g*.

11 200 micrograms/minute = 0.2 mg/minute. 0.2 mg/min × 60 min/hr = *12 mg/hr*.

12 250 mg b.d. = 250 mg twice daily = 500 mg/day. Converting to grams: 0.5 g/day for 7 days = *3.5 g*.

13 2 tablets q.d.s. = 2 tablets 4 times daily = *8 tablets/day*.

14 $\frac{500\,ml}{100\,ml/hr}$ = *5 hours*.

15 Dose prescribed = 160 mg; dose per measure = 40 mg. $\frac{160}{40}$ × 1 ml = *4 ml* (note: the measure is 1 ml not 6 ml).

16 2.5 hours × 50 ml/hr = *125 ml*.

17 Dose prescribed = 10 mg; dose per measure = 5 mg. $\frac{10}{5}$ × 5 ml = *10 ml*.

18 100 mg/5 ml = 20 mg/ml; volume administered = 0.5 ml. 0.5 ml × 20 mg/ml = *10 mg*.

19 Dose prescribed = 80 mg; dose per measure = 50 mg. $\frac{80}{50}$ × 1 = *1.6 ml* (note: the measure is 1 ml not 2 ml).

20 Dose prescribed = 150 mcg; dose per measure = 400 mg/ml. $\frac{150}{400}$ × 1 = $\frac{15}{40}$ = $\frac{3}{8}$ = 0.375 ml = *0.38 ml* (to the nearest 100th of a ml = to two decimal places.)

21 0.6 mg × 1000 mcg/mg = *600 micrograms*.

22 20 drops per ml; 2 microgram per ml. 20 drops = 2 mcg so 1 drop = *0.1 microgram.*

23 70% w/w means 70 g/100 g: 4 g $\times \frac{70}{100} = \frac{280}{100} = 2.8$ g.

24 20% w/v means 20 g/100 ml: 50 g $\times \frac{20}{100} = \frac{1000}{100} = 10$ g.

25 500 micrograms $\times$ 75 = 0.5 mg $\times$ 75 = *37.5 mg.*

26 $\frac{48}{80} \times 1$ litre cancels to $\frac{6}{10} \times 1$ L = 0.6 L. 0.6 L per 8 hours = 600 ml/8 hr = *75 ml/hr.*

27 0.5 mg/min $\times$ 60 min/hr $\times$ 6 hr = 5 $\times$ 6 $\times$ 6 mg = *180 mg.*

28 600 mg $\div$ 3 doses = 200 mg; $\frac{200}{50} \times 5$ ml = *20 ml.*

29 25 000 units in 1.0 ml and we have 0.2 ml. $\frac{0.2}{1.0} \times 25\ 000 = \frac{2}{10} \times$ 25 000 = 2 $\times$ 2500 = *5000 units.*

30 100 mcg/kg/hr $\times$ 60 kg $\times$ 12 mcg = 1000 $\times$ 6 $\times$ 12 mcg = 72 mg. Stock: 10 mg/ml; 72 mg $\div$ 10 mg/ml = *7.2 ml.*

31 1.5 mg $\div$ 4 = 0.375 mg.

$$\frac{0.\ 3\ 7\ 5}{4\ \overline{|1.^{1}5^{3}0^{2}0}}$$

32 Dose prescribed = 1 g; dose per measure = 1.2 g. $\frac{1}{1.2} \times 20$ ml $= \frac{20}{1.2} = \frac{200}{12} = \frac{100}{6} = \frac{50}{3} = 16\frac{2}{3} = 16.667 = $ *16.7 ml* to one decimal place.

33 200 doses $\times$ 400 microgram/dose = 200 $\times \frac{400}{1000}$ mg = 200 $\times \frac{4}{10}$ mg = 20 $\times$ 4 mg = *80 mg.*

34 5 mg/kg $\times$ 80 kg = 400 mg. Stock is 200 mg tablets = *2.*

35 We have 5 ml $\times$ 96 mg/ml = 480 mg in 125 ml of fluid. Dose = 8 mg/min = $\frac{8}{480} \times 125$ ml/min = $\frac{1}{60} \times 125 = \frac{125}{60}$ ml/min = *125 ml/hr.*

36 100 micrograms $\times$ 24 $\times$ 3 = 100 $\times$ 72 = 7200 microgram = *7.2 mg.*

37 1 g per 40 minutes = 1000 mg/40 min = $\frac{1000}{40} = \frac{100}{4} = $ *25 mg/min.*

38 1 ml/min = 1 $\times$ 60 $\times$ 24 ml/day = 1440 ml/day = *1.44 L/day.*

39 0.2% = 0.2 g/100 ml = 200 mg/100 ml = 2 mg/ml. Rewrite this as 4 mg/2 ml. Rate = 4 mg/min = 2 ml/min = *120 ml/hr.*

40 14 drops in 30 seconds = 28 drops/minute. We have 20 drops per ml giving set = $\frac{28\ \text{drops/min}}{20\ \text{drop/ml}} = \frac{14}{10}$ ml/min = 1.4 ml/min. (Check: 1.4 $\times$ 20 = 28.) Multiply by 60 minutes to give ml/hour: 1.4 ml/min $\times$ 60 min/hr = 14 $\times$ 6 ml/hr = 84 ml/hr. 84 ml/hr $\times$ 12 hr = 1008 ml = *1 L approx.*

41   500 mg/50 ml = *10 mg/ml.*

42 $\frac{800}{4000}$ × 100 ml = $\frac{8}{40}$ × 100 = $\frac{8}{4}$ × 10 ml = *20 ml.* Check: 800 mg is one-fifth of 4 g. One-fifth of 100 ml = 20 ml.

43   800 micrograms × 100 = 80 000 micrograms = 80 mg. 80 mg ÷ 80 kg = *1 mg/kg.*

44 $\frac{40}{100}$ = 0.4 mg/ml = *400 micrograms/ml.*

45   5 × 0.8 g/day = 4 g/day. 4 g per day for 7 days = *28 g.*

46   1.5 L = 1500 ml; 1500 ml ÷ 10 hr = 150 ml/hr. 150 ml/hr ÷ 60 min/hr = 2.5 ml/min; 2.5 × 20 = *50 dpm.*

47   150 mg per 24 hours. $\frac{150}{24}$ = $\frac{75}{12}$ = $\frac{25}{4}$ = $6\frac{1}{4}$ = *6.25 mg/hr.*

48   28 + 22 = 50 units/day. Stock is 100 units/ml × 10 ml = 1000 units. 1000 ÷ 50 = *20 days supply.*

49   60 dpm ÷ 20 = 3 ml/min; 3 ml/min × 60 min = 180 ml/hr. 180 ml/hr × 12 hr = 2160 ml = *2.16 L.* (Check: 180 × 12 = 180 × 10 + 180 × 2 = 1800 + 360 = 2160.)

50   Dose prescribed = 1 mg; dose per measure = 1 g = 1000 mg. $\frac{1}{1000}$ × 10 000 = *10 ml.* (Check: 1 g/10 000 ml = 1000 mg/10 000 ml = 1 mg/10 ml.)

Answers to mock test 2

See also the expanded answers which follow.

1	300 mg	26	300 mg
2	650 mg	27	216 mg
3	1.5 mg	28	200 mg
4	1 g	29	8 hours
5	3125 micrograms	30	1.44 g
6	1 mg	31	3 bags
7	30 ml	32	5 ml
8	2 ampoules	33	5 ml
9	2 mg/ml	34	8.4 g
10	5 days	35	25.8 ml
11	5 micrograms/min	36	2.5 mg/ml
12	6 tablets	37	40 micrograms/ml
13	2130 hours	38	20 mg
14	16 ml	39	8 mg/L
15	42 ml	40	1.67 vials
16	$16\frac{2}{3}$ ml/min	41	10 ml
17	80 ml/hr	42	12.5 ml
18	20 ml	43	100 mg/ml
19	1.7 ml	44	2 mg
20	0.35 ml	45	50 drops/min
21	300 mg	46	12 doses
22	0.18%	47	125 mg
23	12.5 g	48	4.2 mg/hr
24	100 mg	49	15 days
25	5 hrs 33 mins	50	30 ml/hr

Mock test 2 expanded answers

1   1.2 g = 1200 mg; 1200 mg ÷ 4 = *300 mg.*

2   50 + 100 + 200 + 300 = *650 mg.*

3   0.0015 g = 0.0015 × 1000 mg = *1.5 mg.*

4   250 mg × 4 = *1 g.*

5   3.125 mg × 1000 mcg/mg = *3125 micrograms.*

6   500 micrograms × 2 = *1 mg.*

7   Dose prescribed = 90 mg; dose per measure = 15 mg. $\frac{90}{15}$ × 5 ml = 6 × 5 ml = *30 ml.*

8   Dose prescribed = 200 mg; dose per measure = 20 mg. $\frac{200}{20}$ × 1 ml = 10 ml = *2 ampoules.*

9   20 mg per 10 ml = $\frac{20}{10}$ = *2 mg/ml.*

10 $\frac{300}{50}$ × 5 = 30 ml; 150 ml ÷ 30 ml/day = *5 days supply.*

11 $\frac{7.2 \times 1000}{24 \times 60} = \frac{72 \times 10}{24 \times 6} = 3 \times \frac{10}{6} = 5$ *microgram/min.*

12 $\frac{18}{6}$ × 3 = 2 × 3 = *6 tablets.*

13 1.5 L = 1500 ml; $\frac{1500\,ml}{120\,ml/hr} = \frac{150}{12} = \frac{50}{4} = \frac{25}{2} = 12.5$ *hr.* Finishes at 0900 + 1230 = *2130 hours.*

14 Dose prescribed = 400 mg; dose per measure = 500 mg. $\frac{400}{500}$ × 20 ml = $\frac{4}{5}$ × 20 = 4 × 4 = *16 ml.*

15 12 hours = 12 × 60 minutes = 720 minutes. $\frac{30}{270}$ × 1000 = $\frac{3}{27}$ × 1000 = $\frac{1}{24}$ × 1000 = $\frac{100}{24} = \frac{500}{12} = \frac{250}{6} = \frac{125}{3}$ = 41.667 = *42 ml* to the nearest ml.

Alternative method: 1 L over 12 hours = $\frac{1000}{12}$ ml/hr. We have 30 minutes = $\frac{1}{2}$ hr; $\frac{1}{2} \times \frac{1000}{12} = \frac{500}{12}$ etc.

16 $\frac{250}{12} = \frac{50}{3} = 16\frac{2}{3}$ ml/min.

17 120 ml in 1.5 hours = $\frac{120}{1.5}$ = *80 ml/hr.* Check: 80 × 1.5 = 120. Alternative method: 120 × $\frac{60}{90}$ = 120 × $\frac{2}{3}$ = *80 ml/hr.*

18 Dose prescribed = 500 mg; dose per measure = 125 mg. $\frac{500}{125}$ × 5 ml = 4 × 5 ml = *20 ml.*

19 Dose prescribed = 20 mg; dose per measure = 30 mg. $\frac{20}{30}$ × 5 ml = $\frac{2}{3}$ × 5 ml = $\frac{10}{3}$ = 3.33. Not used = 5 ml stock – 3.3 ml dose = *1.7 ml.*

20 'Dose' = 35 Units; 'dose per measure' = 100 Units. $\frac{35}{100}$ × 1 = *0.35 ml.*

21 2% w/v = 2 g/100 g. 15 g × $\frac{2}{100} = \frac{30}{100}$ = 0.3 g = *300 mg.*

22 $0.9\% \div 5 = 0.18\%$; alternative: $0.9\% \times \frac{1}{5} = 0.18\%$.

23 50% w/v $= 50$ g/100 ml. 50 g $\times \frac{25\,ml}{100\,ml} = \frac{25}{2} = 12.5\,g$.
Alternative method: 50 g/100 ml $= 0.5$ g/ml; 0.5 g/ml $\times 25$ ml
$= 12.5\,g$.

24 5 mg/kg $\times 60$ kg $= 300$ mg daily in divided doses every
8 hours $= 3$ doses of *100 mg.*

25   60 drops per minute $= 3$ ml/minute. 1 L $= 1000$ ml. $\frac{1000}{3} =$
333.33 minutes $= 5$ hours and 33 minutes (to the nearest
minute).

26 30 mg/ml $\times 10$ ml $= 300\,mg.$

27 $5 \times 72 \times 10 \times \frac{60}{1000} = 5 \times 72 \times \frac{6}{10} = 30 \times \frac{72}{10} = 3 \times 72 = 216\,mg.$

28 450 mg $- 250$ mg $= 200\,mg.$

29 5 mg $= 5000$ micrograms at a rate of 10 mcg/hr. $\frac{5000}{10} = 500$
minutes $= \frac{500}{60}$ hours $= \frac{50}{6}$ hr $= 8\frac{1}{3}$ hr $= 8\,hr$ to the nearest
hour.

30 $20 \times 50 \times 60 \times \frac{24}{1000} = 2 \times 5 \times 6 \times 24 = 10 \times 6 \times 24 = 6 \times$
$240 = 1440$ mg $= 1.44\,g.$

31   Dose prescribed $= 500$ mg/8 hours $= 1.5$ g/day. We have
5 mg/ml in 100 ml bags so dose per bag $= 5$ mg $\times 100 =$
500 mg $= 0.5$ g. 1.5 g $\div 0.5$ g $= 3\,bags$ per day.

32   Dose prescribed $= 20$ mg; dose per measure $= 4$ mg. $\frac{20}{4} \times$
1 ml $= 5 \times 1$ ml $= 5\,ml.$

33   Dose prescribed $= 500$ mg; dose per measure $= 100$ mg.
$\frac{500}{100} \times 1$ ml $= 5 \times 1$ ml $= 5\,ml.$

34   400 mg three times per day for 1 week. 400 mg $\times 3$/day $=$
1.2 g/day; 1.2 g/day $\times 7$ days $= 8.4\,g.$

35   Dose prescribed $= 150 \times 86$ micrograms. Dose per measure
$= 500$ micrograms. $150 \times \frac{86}{500} = 15 \times \frac{86}{50} = 3 \times \frac{86}{10} = 25.8\,ml.$

36 0.25% w/v $= 0.25$ g/100 ml $= 250$ mg/100 ml $= 2.5\,mg/ml.$

37 $20 \times \frac{1000}{500} = 20 \times 2 = 40\,micrograms/ml.$

38 $\frac{4}{24} \times 120 = \frac{1}{6} \times 120 = \frac{120}{6} = 20\,mg.$
Alternative method: 120 mg/24 hr $= \frac{120}{24} = \frac{60}{12} = 5$ mg/hr;
5 mg/hr $\times 4$ hr $= 20\,mg.$

39 500 mcg/ml $\times 2 \times 4$ ml $= 4000$ micrograms $= 4$ mg. 4 mg/
500 ml $= 8$ mg/1000 ml $= 8\,mg/L.$

40 Dose prescribed = 1 g = 1000 mg. Dose per measure = 600 mg. $\frac{1000}{600}$ vials = $\frac{10}{6}$ = $\frac{5}{3}$ = $1\frac{2}{3}$ = *1.67 vials* to two decimal places.

41 Dose prescribed = 500 mg. Dose per measure = 5 g = 5000 mg. $\frac{500}{5000} \times 100 = \frac{1}{10} \times 100 = 10\ ml$. (Check: 500 mg is one-tenth of 5 g. One-tenth of 100 ml = 10 ml.)

42 Dose prescribed = 500 mg. Dose per measure = 4 g = 4000 mg. $\frac{500}{4000} \times 100 = \frac{5}{40} \times 100 = \frac{50}{4} = 12.5\ ml$.

43 750 mg ÷ 7.5 ml = $\frac{7500}{75}$ mg/ml = *100 mg/ml.*

44 $\frac{0.05\ ml}{15\ ml} \times 600 = 5 \times \frac{6}{15} = \frac{6}{3} = 2\ mg$.
Alternative method: 600 mg per 15 ml = $\frac{600}{15}$ = 40 mg/ml; we have 0.05 ml: 0.05 ml × 40 mg/ml = *2 mg*.

45 600 ml/4 hr = 150 ml/hr = $\frac{150}{60}$ ml/min = $\frac{15}{6}$ = 2.5 ml/min; 2.5 ml/min × 20 drops per minute (dpm) = 25 × 2 = *50 dpm.*

46 50 micrograms/ml × 60 ml/bottle = 50 × 60 mcg/bottle. Doses are 250 mcg each: = 50 × $\frac{60}{250}$ doses/bottle = 1 × $\frac{60}{5}$ = *12 doses* per bottle.

47 $\frac{2.5}{10} \times 500 = 2.5 \times 50 = 25 \times 5 = 125\ mg$.
Alternative method: 500 mg per 10 ml of solution: $\frac{500}{10}$ = 50 mg/ml and we have 2.5 ml; 2.5 × 50 = *125 mg.*

48 100 mg per 24 hours: $\frac{100}{24} = \frac{50}{12} = \frac{25}{6} = 4.166 = 4.2\ mg/hr$ to one decimal place.

49 100 units/ml × 3 ml × 2 pens = 600 units. 20 units twice daily = 40 units/day. $\frac{600}{40} = \frac{60}{4} = 15\ days\ supply$.

50 1 mg/minute = 60 mg/hour. 1 g lignocaine/500 ml = 1000 mg/ 500 ml = 2 mg/ml. Take a 1 hour period to simplify the working out, then dose in this time = 60 mg and volume in this time = 60 mg ÷ 2 mg/ml = 30 ml. So infusion rate = 30 ml in 1 hour = *30 ml/hr.*

Answers to mock test 3

See also the expanded answers which follow.

1	5 days supply	**26**	10 mg/hr
2	62.5 micrograms	**27**	0.8 ml
3	3 tablets	**28**	0.4 ml
4	600 ml	**29**	1200 units/hr
5	4 ml	**30**	2 ml/hr
6	400 mg	**31**	4 g
7	2 ml	**32**	150 mg
8	90 mg	**33**	10 mg
9	331.2 mg	**34**	0.24 g
10	10 ml	**35**	15 ml
11	2.5 ml/minute	**36**	72 ml/hr
12	0.12 ml	**37**	120 ml/hr
13	1.2 g	**38**	4 ml/hr
14	1 hour 40 minutes	**39**	1.44 mg/day
15	3 bottles	**40**	17 drops/minute
16	5 mg	**41**	500 microgram/ml
17	3 ml	**42**	8 mg/ml
18	100 micrograms	**43**	1.9 g
19	6 ml	**44**	22 kg
20	22.5 ml	**45**	1.12 g
21	15 ml	**46**	0.8 ml
22	4.5 g	**47**	10 ml
23	1.8 g	**48**	6 ml
24	30 mmol	**49**	4.8 ml
25	4 graduations	**50**	30 ml/hr

Mock test 3 expanded answers

1 First step: calculate the daily dose in millilitres. Dose prescribed = 1 g per day = 1000 mg. Dose per measure = 250 mg. $\frac{100}{250} \times 5$ ml = 4×5 ml = 20 ml per day.

First step: calculate how long the 100 ml bottle will last: 100 ml ÷ 20 ml/day = *5 days supply*.

2 $0.0625 \times 1000 = $ *62.5 micrograms*.

3 1.2 g ÷ 2 doses = 0.6 g = 600 mg/dose. Tablets are 200 mg each; 600 mg ÷ 200 mg/tablet = *3 tablets*.

4 First step: work out the volume of one dose. Dose prescribed = 20 mg; dose per measure = 10 mg. Volume = $\frac{20}{10} \times 5$ ml = 2×5 ml = 10 ml per dose.

Second step: calculate the volume of one bottle. One bottle contains 30 doses = 30×10 ml = 300 ml. So two full bottles contain *600 ml*.

5 20 mg/kg $\times$ 16 kg = 320 mg in two divided doses = 160 mg/dose. Stock is 200 mg/5 ml. Dose prescribed = 160 mg; dose per measure = 200 mg. $\frac{160}{200} \times 5$ ml = $\frac{16}{20} \times 5$ ml = $\frac{4}{5} \times 5$ ml = *4 ml*.

6 2 mg/ml $\times$ 200 ml = *400 mg*.

7 3% w/v = 3 g/100 ml = 3000 mg/100 ml = 30 mg/ml. For a dose of 60 mg: 60 mg ÷ 30 mg/ml = *2 ml*.

8 15 ml $\times \frac{30\ mg}{5\ ml}$ = 3×30 mg = *90 mg*.

Alternative method: 30 mg/5 ml = 6 mg/ml and we have 15 ml; $15 \times 6 = $ *90 mg*.

9 5 micrograms/kg/minute for 12 hours = $\frac{5 \times 92 \times 12 \times 60}{1000}$ mg = $\frac{460 \times 720}{1000}$ mg = $\frac{46 \times 72}{10}$ = 3312 ÷ 10 = *331.2 mg*.

10 2% = 2 g/100 ml = 2000 mg/100 ml = 20 mg/ml. Max dose of 200 mg ÷ 20 mg/ml = *10 ml*.

11 Dose prescribed = 300 mg; dose per measure = 30 mg. $\frac{300}{30} \times 1$ ml = 10×1 ml = 10 ml (full syringe). Given over 4 minutes = *2.5 ml/minute*.

12 12 units of 100 units/ml strength: $\frac{12}{100} \times 1$ ml = *0.12 ml*.

13 Concentration of Tegretol = 100 mg/5 ml = 20 mg/ml. One 20 ml dose contains 20 ml $\times$ 20 mg/ml = 400 mg. t.d.s. = 3 doses per day = 3×400 mg = *1.2 g daily*.

14 1000 mcg ÷ 10 mcg/min = 100 min = *1 hr 40 min.*

15 75 ml/hr × 20 hrs = 1500 ml. 1500 ml ÷ 500 ml/bottle = *3 bottles.*

16 0.5% means 0.5 g/100 ml = 500 mg/100 ml = *5 mg in 1 ml.*

17 Dose prescribed = 2 mg/kg × 22.5 kg = 45 mg. Dose per measure = 75 mg. $\frac{45}{75}$ × 5 ml = $\frac{45}{15}$ ml = *3 ml.*

18 1 in 10 000 means 1 g/10 000 ml = 1000 mg/10 000 ml = 0.1 mg/ml = *100 micrograms in 1 ml.*

19 Dose prescribed = 300 mg; dose per measure = 500 mg. $\frac{300}{500}$ × 10 ml = *6 ml.*

20 Loading dose = 15 mg × 60 = 900 mg. Maintenance dose = 75 mg t.d.s. = 75 × 3 = 225 mg/day. Total = 900 + 225 = 1125 mg. Stock = 50 mg/ml. $\frac{1125}{50}$ × 1 ml = $\frac{2250}{100}$ = *22.5 ml.* (The top and bottom of the fraction have been doubled to give a denominator of 100, which is easier to divide by.)

21 1.25 mg/hr × 24 hr = 30 mg. $\frac{30}{2}$ × 1 ml = *15 ml.*

22 0.9% w/v = 0.9 g/100 ml. So a 500 ml pack contains: $\frac{500}{100}$ × 0.9 g = 5 × 0.9 g = *4.5 g.*

23 0.18% w/v = 0.18 g/100 ml = 1.8 g/1000 ml = *1.8 g.*

24 A 0.18% solution is only one-fifth the concentration of a 0.9% solution: 0.9% ÷ 5 = 0.18% (check: 0.18 × 5 = 0.9). 150 mmol ÷ 5 = *30 mmol.*
Alternative method: $\frac{0.18}{0.9}$ × 15 mmol = $\frac{18}{90}$ × 150 = $\frac{1}{5}$ × 150 = *30 mmol.*

25 1.5 mg/kg × 60 kg = 90 mg. Stock is 100 mg/ml × 1 ml = 100 mg. Wasted = 100 − 90 = 10 mg. 10 ÷ 2.5 = 4 graduations wasted = *4.*

26 Lock-out time = 6 minutes, which gives a maximum of 10 bolus doses per hour of 1 ml each. Each ml contains 1 mg: 1 mg/dose × 10 doses/hr = *10 mg/hr.*

27 Bolus dose = 20 mcg; dose per measure = 25 mcg. $\frac{20}{25}$ × 1 ml = $\frac{4}{5}$ × 1 ml = *0.8 ml.*

28 $\frac{10\,000}{25\,000}$ × 1 ml = $\frac{10}{25}$ = $\frac{2}{5}$ = *0.4 ml.*

29 (5 × 2) + (4 × 1) + 0.4 = 14.4. ml. 14.4 ml × 1000 units/ml = 14 400 units. 24 ml given at a rate of 2 ml/hr: time = 24 ml ÷ 2 ml/hr = 12 hours. Dose rate = 14 400 units ÷ 12 hours = *1200 units/hr.*

30   Stock = 5 ml × 5000 units/ml = 25 000 units. Time = 25 000 units ÷ 1000 units/hr = 25 hours. Infusion rate = 50 ml in 25 hours = *2 ml/hr.*

31   50 mg/kg × 82 kg = 100 × 41 = 4100 mg = 4.1 g which exceeds the maximum daily dose of 4 g, so *4 g.*

32   15% = 15 g/100 ml = 0.15 g/ml = 0.15 × 1000 mg/ml = 150 mg/ml; so 1 ml contains *150 mg.*

33   5 mg t.d.s. = 5 mg three times daily = 15 mg/day; 5 mg tdd = 5 mg total daily dose = 5 mg/day. Difference per day = 15 mg – 10 mg = *10 mg.*

34 $\frac{10}{5}$ × 120 mg = 2 × 120 mg = 240 mg = *0.24 g.* Alternative method: 120 mg/5 ml = $\frac{120}{5}$ = 24 mg/ml. We have 10 ml: 10 ml × 24 mg/ml = 240 mg = *0.24 g.*

35   3.054 g = 3054 mg = two doses 1527 mg each. Dose prescribed = 1527 mg; dose per measure = 509 mg. $\frac{1527}{509}$ × 5 ml = 3 × 5 = 15 ml.

36   Stock: 25 mg/ml 10 ml amp; it contains 25 × 10 = 250 mg. 250 mg in 500 ml of infusion fluid = $\frac{250}{500}$ = 0.5 mg/ml. Rate = 36 mg/hr; take one hour for ease of working out. Dose = 36 mg; then volume = 36 mg ÷ 0.5 mg/ml = 72 ml in one hour, which is *72 ml/hr.*

37   The pump is on from 2200 to 0700 = 9 hours. The first 4 hours (2200 to 0200 hrs) at 100 ml/hr = 400 ml. This leaves 5 hours for the remaining 600 ml. 600 ml ÷ 5 hours = *120 ml/hr.*

38   0.1 units/kg/hr × 40 kg = 4 units/hr. We have 50 units/50 ml = 1 unit/ml (units/hr = ml/hour) so 4 units/hr = *4 ml/hr.*

39   1 microgram per minute = $\frac{1 \times 60 \times 24}{1000}$ mg/day = $\frac{144}{100}$ mg/day = *1.44 mg/day.*

40   500 ml in 10 hours with a 20 drops/ml giving set: $\frac{500 \times 20}{10 \times 60}$ = $\frac{50 \times 2}{1 \times 6}$ = $\frac{100}{6}$ = $16\frac{2}{3}$ = *17 dpm.*

41   0.05% w/v = 0.05 g/100 ml = 50 mg/100 ml = 0.5 mg/ml = *500 micrograms/ml.*

42   Strength = $\frac{40\,mg}{5\,ml}$ = *8 mg/ml.*

43   50 mg/kg × 38 kg = 1900 mg = *1.9 g.*

44   Weight in kg = 2 × (age + 4). For a seven-year-old = 2 × (7 + 4) = 2 × 11 = *22 kg.*

45 20 mg once daily for 8 weeks: 20 mg $\times$ 7 $\times$ 8 = 20 mg/day $\times$ 56 days = 10 $\times$ 112 = 1120 mg = *1.12 g.*

46 Volume of solution = 5 ml. Volume of water added to powder = 4.2. Difference = 5.0 − 4.2 = *0.8 ml* the volume displaced by the powder.

47 9.7 ml + 0.3 ml = *10 ml.*

48 9.5 ml + 0.5 ml = 10 ml. Dose prescribed = 300 mg; dose per measure = 500 mg. $\frac{300}{500} \times 10$ ml = $\frac{3}{5} \times 10$ ml = 3 $\times$ 2 ml = *6 ml.*

49 5.5 ml + 0.5 ml = 6 ml. Dose prescribed = 600 mg; dose per measure = 750 mg. $\frac{600}{750} \times 6$ ml = $\frac{60}{75} \times 6 = \frac{4}{5} \times 6 = \frac{24}{5}$ = *4.8 ml.*

50 10 micrograms/kg/min = 10 $\times$ 80 = 800 micrograms/min. Converting to mg = 0.8 mg/min. Stock = 2 $\times$ 10 ml $\times$ 40 mg/ml = 800 mg. Dividing the stock by the rate of consumption gives the time: 800 mg $\div$ 0.8 mg/min = 8000 $\div$ 8 = 1000 minutes. 500 ml solution in 1000 minutes = 0.5 ml/min = *30 ml/hr.*

Nursing abbreviations and key words

Abbreviations – *Yes* √

1 You can use abbreviations informally for note-taking purposes during handovers, as shown in the example below.

> *Mary Jones 75, TCI. Hx AF, IHD, SOB, CVA rt-hemi.*
> *↑ D-dimer. VQ scan for PE NAD. NBM, Rx IV AB for UTI*

Patient Mary Jones, age 75, was a planned admission (TCI – to come in). History of AF (atrial fibrillation), IHD (ischaemic heart disease), SOB (shortness of breath), CVA (cerebro-vascular accident – a stroke) with a right-sided hemi (hemiperesis – weakness). Has a raised D-dimer (positive test for a blood clot). VQ scan (lung ventilation-perfusion) for a PE (pulmonary embolism) was NAD (no abnormalities detected). NBM (nil by mouth) Rx (prescribed) IV AB (intravenous antibiotics) for a UTI (urinary tract infection).

2 You can use abbreviations in formal work only after the full terms have been written out with the abbreviated form in brackets, as shown in the example below.

A cerebro-vascular accident (CVA) can be either haemorrhagic or ischaemic. Mrs Jones CVA was haemorrhagic, ie a bleed.

3 You can use abbreviations that find widespread use, are well known or are units of measure, eg NHS, NMC, UK, BSc, mg, ml, etc.

4 You can use abbreviations that are part of an approved list for you workplace.

Abbreviations – $\mathcal{N}o$ ✗

1 Avoid using abbreviations in patient's nursing notes and especially in important documentation (eg consent forms, incident reports).

2 Avoid using abbreviation that could be misconstrued. Some abbreviations mean different things to different people, for example, RTS could mean respiratory tract secretions to a nurse and a raised toilet seat to an occupational therapist.

3 Avoid using abbreviations in transfer of care or discharge documentation. 'NSTEMI' might be understood in coronary care but not when the patient is transferred to rehab.

4 Avoid using less familiar chemical symbols or formula (eg Fe, $FeSO_4$). However, the symbols for the common electrolytes can normally be used, eg Na^+, K^+, Ca^{2+} and Cl^-.

5 Never abbreviate micrograms to mcg or ug, and do not abbreviate units (insulin) to U or International Units to IU.

6 Avoid using am and pm with clock times; always use the 24-hour clock.

The following list contains over 600 abbreviations, many of which come with a short explanation. The list is not exhaustive, so you will come across additional abbreviations on the wards or in the community.

Numbers and symbols

1/7 (once a day), 1/52 (once a week), 1/12 (once a month)
< (less than) and > (more than) can be confusing, so avoid;
= (equal to)
5-FU (5-fluorosil, a chemotherapy drug used to treat cancer)
(fracture of bone, eg # NOF)
+ (present); ++ (present a lot); +++ (present to excess)
+ve (positive) and -ve (negative): use pos and neg instead
? (query)
@ (at).

Alphabetical list

AA – aplastic anaemia (a rare condition where the bone marrow fails to produce enough red blood cells)

AAA – abdominal aortic aneurism (ballooning of the aorta due to a weakened artery wall)

AAD – antibiotic associated diarrhoea

A&A – aids and appliances

A&E – accident and emergency department

A&P – anatomy and physiology

ABCDE of life support (airways, breathing, circulation, disability (eg diabetes, drugs (GCS)), exposure (head to toe))

Abd. – abdominal

abdo – abdomen

ABGs – arterial blood gases (see also SATs)

ABI – acquired brain injury (head injury)

ABMT – autologous bone marrow transplant (taken from another part of the patient's body)

ABO – blood group system

ABPI – ankle-brachial pressure index (dopper results)

ABX – antibiotic

ACE – angiotensin converting enzyme (eg ACE inhibitor drugs)

ACS – acute coronary syndromes. Unstable angina or NSTEMI.

AD – Alzheimer's disease

ADH – anti-diuretic hormone (pituitary gland; urine decreased)

ADHD – attention deficit hyperactivity disorder

ADLs – activities of daily living (see also ALs)

ADR – adverse drug reaction; a medication that has an unintended, harmful affect when given as a normal dose

AF – atrial fibrillation (abnormal heart rhythm (arrhythmia) linked to a faulty SA node)

AFC – Agenda for change

Ag – the chemical symbol for silver

AIDS – acquired immune deficiency syndrome

AIR – adverse incident report

AK – actinic keratosis – pre-cancerous spots (UVdamage); SCC

AKA – 1. above knee amputation; 2. also known as

Al – the chemical symbol for aluminium

Alb. – albumin

ALs – activities of living (same as ADLs)

AMAU – acute medical admissions unit

AMI – acute myocardial infarction. A heart attack.

AML – acute myeloid leukaemia

Amnio – amniocentesis (diagnostic test on fetus)

amp – ampule

Anaes. – anaesthetic

ANS – autonomic nervous system

ANP – Advanced Nurse Practitioner

Anti-D – immunolobin treatment for pregnant women

ANTT – antiseptic non touch technique

APPT – activated partial thromboplastin time. A measure of the blood's ability to coagulate. Normally 30 to 45 seconds.

ARDS – acute respiratory distress syndrome

ARF – acute renal failure

ASA – acetyl salicylic acid. Aspirin

ASAP – as soon as possible

ATP – adenosine triphosphate (the energy carrying molecule)

ATLS – advanced trauma life support

AV node – atrioventricular node (delays electrical impulse so that the ventricles contract momentarily after the atria)

AVPU – Alert (awake); Voice; (responds to), Pain (responds to); unresponsive; see also GCS

Ax – assessment

AXR – abdominal X-ray

Ba – the chemical symbol for barium

BaE – Bariun enema (used when X-raying the colon; a barium drink is used when X-raying the stomach and upper GI tract)

BB – bed bath

BBB – bundle branch block (a failure in the heart's conduction system; visible in an ECG)

BC – blood cultures

BCC – basal cell carcinoma (invasive growth that rarely metasta-sizes; also known as a rodent ulcer)

BCG – Bacilli Calmette Guerin. A TB vaccine for the newborn

BD – Bowen's disease (non-invasive squamous cell carcinoma)

bd/bid – twice a day (Latin)

BG – blood glucose (see also BM); normal range is 4.0 to 7.8 (mmol/l); hypoglycaemia is 3.0 or below; diagnosis of diabetes is 11.0 mmol following a glucose challenge (see OGTT)

BIBA – brought in by ambulance

bid – see bd (twice daily)

BiPAP – Bilevel positive airway pressure (oxygen supplied under pressure (via a face mask) to assist breathing)

BKA – below knee amputation

BLS – basic life support (see also ABCDE)

BM – blood glucose monitoring (named after Boehringer Mannheim of German, manufacturer of glucometers)

BMA – British Medical Association

BME – black and minority ethnic

BMI – body mass index (patients weight in kg divided by the patients height in metres squared; eg weight 65 kg, height 1.6 m; BMI = $65 \div 1.6^2 = 25.4$ (alternatively: $65 \div 1.6 \div 1.6 = 25.4$))

BMR – basal metabolic rate (the amount of calories your body needs when resting)

BNF – *British National Formulary* (medical reference book listing the medicines and dressings available on the NHS)

BNO – bowels not opened

BO – bowels opened

BOR – bowels opened regularly

Borg scale – breathlessness (dyspnoea) on a scale from 0 to 10

BP – arterial blood pressure (systolic/diastolic)

BPD – biparietal diameter. Baby's head diameter.

BPH – benign prostatic hypertrophy (enlarged prostate)

BPM – beats per minute (heart rate)

BS – bowel sounds; breath sounds

BSA – body surface area

BWO – bowels well opened

Bx – biopsy (removal of a tissue sample from the body)

C – Celcius. Temperature measuring scale (see also T)

CA/ca. – carcinoma/cancer

Ca. – the chemical symbol for calcium

CABG – coronary artery bypass graft (the saphenous vein is taken from the leg and stitched to the aorta)

CAD – coronary artery disease (see IHD)

CAIR – critical adverse incident report

Cal – calories (non-SI unit measurement of energy; 1 cal = 4.2 joules (J), which is the SI unit (metric system))

CAPD – continuous ambulatory peritoneal dialysis (see PD)

caps – capsules

C&S – culture and sensitivity (bacteria from infected tissue, urine or blood are grown in a medium (cultured) to determine which antibiotics can fight the bacteria)

CAT scan – computerized axial tomography scan

cath – catheter

CAUTI – catheter associated UTI

CBC – capillary blood count

CBG – capillary blood glucose

CCB – calcium channel blocker (a class of medication)

CCF – congestive cardiac failure (may be acute or CHF)

CCR – creatine clearance rate (measures the efficiency of the kidneys to filter creatine from the plasma)

CCU – coronary care unit

CDH – 1. congenital dislocation of the hip; 2. chronic daily headache syndrome

CDs – controlled drugs (eg diamorphine (heroin), morphine, pethedine (all require a lockable CD cupboard and a CD record book; diazepam and midazolam are excluded))

CDiff – *clostridium difficile* (bacterial infection)

CDM – chronic disease management

Ceff and Met – Cephalexine and Metrondiazole antibiotics

Ch – Charriere size (diameter of a catheter)

CHD – coronary heart disease

Chemo – chemotherapy

CHF – chronic heart failure (see also CCF)

CIS – critical illness score (see MEWS and PEWS)

CJD – Creutzfeldt-Jakob disease

CK – creatine kinase (an enzyme detected in a blood test; raised levels are consistent with a heart attack or a stroke)

CKD – chronic kidney disease

CKMB – creatine kinase-MB (an enzyme detected in a blood test; raised levels are consistent with damage to heart muscle)

cm – centimetre

CML – chronic myeloid leukaemia

CN – charge nurse

CNS – central nervous system (the brain and spinal cord)

CO_2 – carbon-dioxide

c/o – complaining of

CO – cardiac output (volume of blood pumped per minute)

C of E – Church of England

Conc – concentration

COPD – chronic obstructive pulmonary disease

COSHH – control of substances hazardous to health

COTE – care of the elderly

CP – cerebral palsy

CPAP – continuous positive airway pressure

CPD – continuing professional development

CPN – community psychiatric nurse

CPR – cardio pulmonary resuscitation

CrCl. – creatine clearance

CRF – chronic renal failure (gradual loss of kidney function)

CRIF – closed reduction with internal fixation (of fracture)

CRP – C-reactive protein (a blood test that is a marker of an inflammatory response linked to an infection)

C/S – Caesarean section

CSF – cerebro-spinal fluid

C-Spine – cervical spine

CSM – circulation, sensation and movement (a check for blood flow and nerve damage to an extremity after injury)

CSU – catheter specimen of urine

CT scan (see CAT scan)

CTPA – CT pulmonary angiography

CTN – call to needle time (see DTN)

CVA – cerebro-vascular accident (a stroke)

CVAD – central venous access device (used to insert a CVL)

CVL – central venous line (a tube placed in the jugular, subclavian or femoral veins for IV access)

CVP – central venous pressure (the blood pressure in the central veins close to the heart; eg raised in heart failure and reduced in hypovolaemic shock)

CXR – chest X-ray

CYTOMEN – refers to Neo-cytamen, which is a trade name for hydroxocobalin (vitamin B12); used with pernicious anaemia

D&C – dilatation and curettage (a gynaecological procedure)

D&F – diet and fluids

D&V – diarrhoea and vomiting

Db – decibel (the unit of sound intensity)

Dc – discharge

DEXA scan – Dual energy X-ray absorptiometry. A scan used to diagnose osteoporosis (loss of bone mass)

DHS – dynamic hip screw

diam – diameter

DIC – disseminated intravascular coagulation (clotting problem)

DKA – diabetic ketoacidosis (ketones when fat is broken down)

DMARD – disease modifying anti-rheumatic drug

DMSA scan – of the kidneys; useful in infants and children with unresolved UTIs

DN – district nurse

DNA – 1. dioxy nucleic acid; 2. did not attend

DNR – do not resuscitate (write this out in full)

DOA – dead on arrival

DOB – date of birth

DOPPLER – ultrasound used to study blood flow (see also ABPI)

DP – dorsalis pedis (one of the pedal pulses used during Doppler studies); see also PT

DRE – digital rectal examination (an examination of the rectum with the finger, eg prior to the use of an enema)

DSH – deliberate self harm

DTN – door to needle time (the time between experiencing symptoms (eg of a CVA, MI) and receipt of IV medication)

DTs – delirium tremens (delirium and tremors linked to alcohol withdrawal)

Dukes A, B, C, D grading system for colorectal cancer (ranging from A (innermost lining only) to D (advanced with metastases)

DVT – deep vein thrombosis. A blood clot in a deep vein

Dx – diagnosis (also Δ)

e – ecstasy drug (MDMA)

EAU – emergency assessment unit

EC – enteric coated (coating applied to a tablet to prevent digestion in the stomach where the medication is an irritant)

ECG – electrocardiogram (detects the hearts electrical impulses and prints out the PQRS and T waves on graph paper)

ECHO – echocardiogram (ultrasound scan of the heart)

E coli – *Escherichia coli* – bacteria found in the gut. Some strains are responsible for food poisoning and UTIs

ED – erectile dysfunction

EDH – extradural haematoma (a bleed in the skull)

EEG – electroencephalogram (displays brain electrical activity)

eg – *exempli gratia* (Latin), for example

EGFR – estimated Glomerular Filtration Rate (see also GFR); venous bloods and 24-hr urine collection; CKD management.

EMI – elderly mentally ill (outdated term for dementia)

EMU – early morning urine sample

ENT – ear, nose and throat

ERCP – endoscopic retrograde choliangio pancreatography (endscopic examination of the pancreas and gall bladder)

ESR – erythrocyte sedimentation rate (blood test measuring the rate at which red blood cells settle – inflammatory marker)

ESRD – end stage renal disease

ESRF – end stage renal failure

EST – exercise stress test (cardiac test, eg on a treadmill)

ETT – endotracheal tube (for intubation; keeps the airway open)

EWS – early warning system (see also MEWS, PEWS and CIS)

EXT – external

FBC – full blood count (red cells, white cells and platelets)

FBG – fasting blood glucose (see FBS)

FBS – fasting blood sugar (a blood glucose test after fasting for at least 8 hours (eg overnight); water and tablets exempted)

FEM-POP – femoral popliteal (bypass). A graft used to bypass arteries in the leg that have become blocked as a result of PVD

FEV1 – forced expiratory volume in 1 second (the rate at which you can breathe out; reduced in COPD)

FiO_2 – fraction of inspired oxygen

FL – femur length (baby's)

Flex. – flexion

FLIP-FLO VALVE – a tap attached directly to a catheter instead of a leg bag so that the bladder fills normally rather than drains

FOB – faecal occult blood – a test for blood (hidden) in the stool

FP10 – prescription drugs/treatments on the NHS formulary that can be dispensed by a pharmacy

Fr – French gauge (see Ch)

FRAT tool – falls risk assessment tool

FRAX tool – fracture risk assessment tool

FROM – full range of movement

FSH – follicle-stimulating hormone

FTND – full term normal delivery

FVC – forced vital capacity (the volume of air that can be breathed out after taking the deepest breath)

FWB – fully weight-bearing

FWT – full ward test. Urinalysis using urine testing sticks

g – gram

GA – general anaesthetic

GABA – Gamma Amino Butyric Acid (an inhibitory neurotransmitter)

G&S – Group and Save (or group and hold/group and screen) – an ABO blood group and antibody-screen blood test taken for patients expected to need a blood transfusion

GCA – giant cell arteritis (inflammed temporal arteries)

GCS – Glasgow Coma Scale (measures neurological function/brain injury on a scale from 3 to 15 (eye opening (1–4), verbal (1–5) and motor (1–6) responses; 7 or less = coma; 8–12 = moderate brain injury; 13–15 = mild brain injury). See also PEARL, AVPU and ABCDE

GFR – glomerular filtration rate (indicates kidney function)

GGT – gamma glutyl transpeptidase (a liver function blood test)

GH – growth hormone

GI – gastrointestinal; GIT – gastrointestinal tract

Glut Max – gluteus maximus muscle

GMC – General Medical Council

GORD – Gastro-oesophageal reflux disease

GP – General Practitioner

GTN – glycerol trinitrate (eg GTN spray/tablets relieve chest pain (angina) by widening the coronary arteries)

GTT – glucose tolerance test (diagnosis of type 2 diabetes)

Gtts – guttae (drops)

GUM – Genitourinary Medicine

GXM – group and cross- match (see X-MATCH)

GYN – gynae, gynaecology

GZM – gutter Zimmer frame

h/hr – hour

HAD scale – hspital anxiety and depression scale

HAI – hospital associated infection

Hartman's – a solution for IV infusion (replenishes electrolytes)

HAV – hepatitis A virus

HBV – hepatitis B virus

Hb – haemoglobin (the oxygen carrier in red blood cells; normal levels are approx 13–17 in men and 12–15 in women; anaemia starts at levels of 11.0 or lower (units: gram/decilitre))

HbA_{1c} – glycosylated haemoglobin (also referred to as the A1c; measures the average blood glucose levels over several weeks; target HbA_{1c} in diabetes is 48 mmol/mol (6.5%)

HCT – haemocrit (the red blood cell count of whole blood)

HCV – hepatitis C virus

HD – haemodialysis (eg in renal failure)

HDL – high-density lipoproteins ('good' cholesterol)

HDU – High Dependency Unit

Hemi – half

Hg – the chemical symbol for mercury

HH – hiatus hernia (a hernia in the chest where the stomach has bulged (herniated) though the wall of the diaphragm)

Hib – Haemophilus Influenza B

HIV – human immunodeficiency virus

HO – house officer (a junior doctor)

H/O – history of (also Hx)

HPHC – high protein/high carbohydrate diet

HR – heart rate

HRT – hormone replacement therapy

Ht. – height

HTN – hypertension

HV – health visitor

HVS – high vaginal swab

Hx – history of (also H/O)

Hypo. – hypoglycaemia (blood glucose below 3.0 mmol/l)

I&O – intake and output (as recorded on a fluid balance chart)

IBS – irritable bowel syndrome

IBD – irritable bowel disease

ICP – 1. intracranial pressure; 2. integrated care pathway

ICU – intensive care unit

ID – infectious disease

IDA – iron deficiency anaemia

IDC – indwelling urinary catheter

IDDM – insulin-dependent diabetes mellitus (Type 1 diabetes)

ie – *id est* (Latin), that is to say

Igs – immunoglobins (IgA, IgG, IgM)

IGT – a test for impaired glucose tollerance

IHD – ischaemic heart disease (fatty deposits narrow the coronary
    arteries, reducing the heart's O^2 supply)

ILS – intermediate life support

IM – intramuscular (eg an injection into muscle)

IM nailing – intramedullary nailing (or IM rod); a metal (titanium) rod
    fixed inside a fractured bone with screws

info. – information

INH – inhaled (eg reliever and preventer medication in COPD)

INR – international normalized ratio (used to monitor the increase in
    blood clotting time with warfarin therapy; eg typical range is
    2–2.5 for atrial fibrillation or DVT prophylaxis)

IPF – idiopathic pulmonary fibrosis (scarring and thickening of the
    lung tissue with no known cause (idiopathic))

in-situ – in its original position

ISC – intermittent self-catheterization

ITU – intensive therapy unit

IU – international unit (avoid this abbreviation)

IUCD – intra-uterine contraceptive device

IV – intravenous (into a vein)

IV AB – intravenous antibiotics

IV bolus – intravenous bolus dose (IV loading dose)

IVF – in-vitro fertilization

IVI – intravenous infusion

IVU – intravenous urogram (X-ray radiography of the kidneys and urology system following an injection of dye)

Ix – investigation

J – joule; SI (metric) unit of energy; see also calorie

JVD – jugular venous distension (consistent with a raised JVP)

JVP – jugular venous pressure (a raised JVP is associated with poor cardiac output)

K – 1. kilo (ie × 1000); 2. K – chemical symbol for potassium

Kcal – kilocalories (1000 calories)

KCl – chemical formula of potassium chloride

kg – kilogram (1000 grams)

KJ – kilojoule (1000 joules)

kPa – kilopascal (metric unit of pressure)

KUB – kidneys, ureter and bladder (x-ray)

KVO – keep vein open

L – litre

LA – local anaesthetic

Lab – laboratory

L&D – labour and delivery (intrapartum)

Lap coli – laparoscopic cholecystectomy (gall bladder removal)

LBBB – left bundle branch block (seen as an abnormal ECG)

lbs. – pounds weight

LD – learning disability

LDL – low density lipoprotein ('bad' cholesterol)

LFT – liver function test (venous bloods taken)

LH – luteinizing hormone (rises before ovulations)

LHS – left-hand side

LIF – left iliac fossa (in the left lower quadrant of the abdomen)

LIH – left inguinal hernia (a hernia in the groin's LHS, where the intestine has bulged (herniated) though the abdominal wall)

LMW – low molecular weight

LN – lymph node

LOC – level of consciousness; loss of consciousness

LOLER – Lifting operations and lifting equipment regulations
LP – lumbar puncture ('spinal tap' to collect cerebrospinal fluid)
L spine – lumbar spine
Lt – left (write out in full)
LTC – long term care
LVAD – left ventricular assistance device
LVF – left ventricular failure
LVH – left ventricular hypertrophy (enlarged heart)
Ly – lying

m^2 – metres squared (surface area)
MAE – medication administration error
Mane – early in the morning (Latin)
MAOI – monoamine oxidase inhibitors
MAP – mean arterial pressure
MARs – Medicine Administration Record sheets
MAU – medical assessment unit
Max – maximum
Maxfac – maxillofacial
MC&S – microscopy culture and sensitivity
mcg – microgram (non-standard abbreviation; also μg)
MCHC – mean cell haemoglobin concentration
MCV – mean corpuscular volume (average red blood cell size)
MDI – metered dose inhaler (eg salbutamol)
MDMA – Ecstasy drug ('e')
MDS – monitored dosage system (eg blister packs for tablets and
    capsules; aids compliance)
MDT – multidisciplinary team
ME – myalgic encephalomyelitis (chronic fatigue syndrome)
Meds (medications)
Mets – metastases; the spread of cancer
MEWS – modified early warning score (illness scoring system which
    uses enhanced standard obs, ie BP, HR, RR and T plus pain
    score, GCS, peak flow, urine output/testing. A score of 5 or more
    is a predictor of a cardiac arrest (seek medical input (eg bleep
    SHO; ECG, O_2 and IV access); also if 3 or more on a single
    reading, or patient deteriorating); MEWS obs if 2 or less

mg – milligram

MI – myocardial infarction. (a heart attack)

MID – multi-infarct dementia (from multiple small strokes)

Mins – minute (unit of time)

min. – minimum

MIU – Minor Injuries Unit

MMR – vaccine measles, mumps and rubella

ml – millilitre (one-thousandth of a litre)

mm – millimetre

mmHg – millimetres of mercury (unit of pressure)

mmol – millimol (one-thousandth of a mole)

MND – motor neurone disease

MSSU 1. see MSU; 2. Medical Short Stay Unit

mol – mole (a mole of any substance contains 6.022×10^{23} atoms or molecules (Avogadro's number)

MONA – Morphine, Oxygen, Nitroglycerin, Aspirin (for an MI)

M/R – modified release (eg capsules)

MRCP – magnetic resonance cholangiopancreatography

MRI (scan) – magnetic resonance imaging

MRSA – methicillin resistant staph aureus bacteria

MS – multiple sclerosis

MSE – maintaining a safe environment

MST – morphine sulphate

MSU – mid-stream specimen of urine. A clean specimen of urine

MUA – manipulation under anaesthetic

MUST tool – Malnutrition Universal Screening Tool

MV – mitralvalve

MVA – motor vehicle accident

MVR – mitral valve replacement

MVT – multi-vitamins (eg prescribed in alcohol-dependency)

Na – the chemical symbol for sodium

NaCl – the chemical formula for sodium chloride

NA – 1. not applicable; 2. non-adhesive (dressing)

NAC – N-acetylecystein (Parvolex); for paracetamol overdose

NAD – no abnormality detected

N&V – nausea and vomiting

NB – nota bene (note well in Latin; i.e. important)

NBI – no bone injury

NBM – nil by mouth (pre- and post-operative fasting)

Nebs – nebulization (an inhaled fine mist)

Neg – negative

NEWS – National Early Warning Score (see MEWS)

NFR – not for resuscitation (see DNR)

NG tube – nasogastric tube (passed down nose into stomach)

NHS – National Health Service

NIC – nurse in charge

NICE – National Institute for Health and Clinical Excellence

NIDDM – non-insulin dependent diabetes mellitus (old term for type 2 diabetes; some patients will eventually require insulin)

NIV – non-invasive ventilation

NJ tube – nasojejunal tube (down nose,to stomach and intestines)

NJR – National Joint Registry (database of personal details)

NKA – no known allergies

NKDA – no known drug allergies

NMR – nuclear magnetic resonance (medical imaging technique)

NNU – Neonatal Unit

Nocte – night

No – number

NOF – neck of femur

NOK – next of kin

NPIS – National Poisons Information Service

NPU – not passed urine

NR – normal range

N/R – night report

NRB – non-re-breather (oxygen) mask

NS – normal saline

NSAID – non-steroidal anti-inflammatory drug

NSF – National Service Framework

NSR – normal sinus rhythm

NSTEMI – non-ST segment elevated myocardial infarction

NTT – nasotracheal tube (a tube inserted via the nose for O_2)

NVD – 1. nausea, vomiting, diarrhoea; 2. natural vaginal delivery

NWB – non-weight-bearing

NYHA – New York Heart Association classification of heart failure (ranges from Class 1, Mild (no SOB) to Class 4, Severe)

O_2 – oxygen

O/A – on admission

OA – osteoarthritis (degenerative disease of the joints ('wear and tear') of the load-bearing joints, eg hips and knees)

OAB – overactive bladder (as in urinary continence)

OAT – oxygen assessment team

OB – occult blood (see FOB)

Obs – observations (baseline obs/observations of progress; eg bp, pulse, resps, temp)

od – once daily (Latin)

OGD – oesophago-gastro-duodenoscopy (a gastroscopy – a camera in a thin tube is passed down the throat of patients with digestive disorders; stomach must be empty for at least 6 hrs)

OGTT – an oral glucose tolerance test (fasting followed by a glucose drink with blood glucose checked 2 hours later)

OM – each morning (meds)

ON – each night (meds)

Onc. – oncology

OOH – out of hours (eg OOH doctor)

OP – osteoporosis (brittle bone disease; notably women over 50)

OPA – Outpatients appointment

OPD – Outpatients Department

OPG – orthopantomogram. An X-ray of the jaw and teeth

ORIF – open reduction with internal fixation (of fracture)

Ortho – orthopaedics

OT – Occupational Therapy/Therapist

PACs – premature atrial contractions

PACS – picture archiving communication system (X-ray images and scan can be viewed on computers)

PACU – post-anaesthetic care unit

PAD – peripheral arterial disease (PAD). Hardening and narrowing of the arteries, especially in the legs. The symptoms are pain in one or both legs on walking

PaO^2 – partial pressure of oxygen

PAP – pulmonary artery pressure

PARS – patient at risk score (see MEWS)

PAEDS – Paediatrics

PCA – patient controlled analgesia (the patient presses the button on the PCA pump to deliver analgesia (eg pethedine) as needs

PCI – Percutaneous Coronary Intervention (opens the coronary artery using a wire mesh tube (stent) or a balloon (angioplasty))

PCT's – Primary Care Trusts

PCV – packed cell volume (percent red blood cells by volume)

PD – 1. Parkinson's disease; 2. Peritoneal dialysis (uses the patient's abdominal membrane as a filter)

PE – pulmonary embolism. A blockage of one or more arteries of the lungs, usually by a clot transported from the deep veins of the leg. Symptoms include chest pain and SOB

PEA – pulseless electrical activity (non-shockable cardiac arrest)

PEARL – pupils equal and reactive to light (one dilated pupil may indicate a head injury or CVA)

PEEP – positive end respiratory pressure (the alveolar pressure above atmospheric pressure; a feature of mechanical ventilation)

PEFR – peak expiratory flow rate

PEG (tube) – percutaneous endoscopic gastrostomy. A flexible tube that goes though the abdominal wall into the stomach for giving liquid food and medications (patient is typically NBM)

PEP – post-exposure prophylaxis (treatment after a needlestick)

PET (scan) – Positron Emission Topography (imaging)

PEWS – Paediatric early warning score (also physiological early warning score; see also MEWS)

PGD – patient group directive (as used to administer vaccines)

pH – acid/alkali scale; from pH 0 (strongest acid) to pH 14 (strongest alkali), with pH 7.0 neutral (pure water); gastric acid approx 1.5 to 3.0; (pH of NG tube aspirate must be less than 5.5)

PHCT – Primary Health Care Team

PHx – past history (of)

Physio – physiotherapist

PICC – peripherally inserted central (venous) catheter

PICU – Paediatric Intensive Care Unit

PKU – Phenylketonuria. A test to reveal an inherited enzyme deficiency that can lead to developmental delay/LD in children

PLN – psychiatric liaison nurse

PMB – post-menopausal bleeding

PMH – past medical history

PMS – premenstrual syndrome

PN – parenteral nutrition (feed given intravenously)

PND – 1. post-natal depression; 2. paroxysmal nocturnal dyspnoea (SOB in the night)

PNE – primary nocturnal enuresis (bedwetting in children)

PNS – peripheral nervous system (the sensory & motor neurons)

PO – per oral (medication by mouth)

PODs – patients' own drugs (own supply brought from home)

POM – prescription only medications (doctor's prescription)

POP – plaster of Paris

pO_2 – the partial pressure of oxygen (0.21 in room air)

post op. – post operation

POVA – protection of vulnerable adults (eg a policy for)

PPI – proton pump inhibitor (drug to reduce gastric acid secretion)

PPM – 1. permanent pace maker; 2. parts per million.

PPX – prophylaxis (a treatment to prevent a problem)

PR – per rectal. As in a PR bleed or PR medication (eg enema)

Pre-med – premedication (eg sedative given before anaesthesia)

Pre op. – pre-operation

PRN – prescription required as needed stock (medication that can be given when needed)

PSA – prostate-specific antigen (level rises in ca prostate)

PT – 1. prothrombin time (a blood test that measures clotting time (coagulation); also used to calculate the INR); 2. posterial tibial (one of the pedal pulses used during a Doppler); see also DP

pt – patient

PTA – post-traumatic amnesia (after a head injury)

PTCA – percutaneous transluminal coronary angioplasty (see also PCI)

PTT – partial thromboplastin time (a blood test used to detect bleeding disorders)

PU – 1. passed urine; 2. pressure ulcer; 3. peptic ulcer

PUD – peptic ulcer disease

PUIT – passed urine in toilet; as used on fluid balance charts

PUVA therapy – Psoralen and ultraviolet A therapy. A treatment for severe psoriasis and other skin disorders that uses UV light

PV – per vagina

PVCs – premature ventricular contractions (beats triggered in the ventricles rather than from the SA node; ectopic (irregular beat))

PVD – peripheral vascular disease (see also PAD)

PWB – partially weight-bearing

Px – 1. prescription; 2. prognosis

Q – every

Q4h – every four hours

QDS – four times daily

QOF – Quality and Outcomes Framework (GP points-based payment system for achieving standards)

QoL – quality of life

QRS wave – (or QRS complex) the tall spike seen on an ECG when the ventricles contract (peak at R)

Quads – quadriceps (large leg muscles for sitting and standing)

R – right

RA – rheumatoid arthritis (chronic autoimmune disorder, which leads to inflammation of the joints bilaterally (women especially)

RAAS – renin angiotensin aldosterone system (regulates BP)

R&D – research and development

Rad. hys. – radical hysterectomy

RAS – 1. rennin-angiotensin system (see RAAS) 2. reticular activating system (the attention centre of the brain; sleep/awake)

RBC count – red blood cell count

RBG – random blood glucose

RC – Roman Catholic

RCN – Royal College of Nursing

RCP – Royal College of Physicians

RCTs – randomized controlled trials

RDAs – recommended daily allowances (of nutrients)

Re. – regarding

Reg. – Registrar (a doctor training in a specialty)

Rehab – rehabilitation

REM – rapid eye movement (in abnormal sleep)

Resps – respiratory rate (see RR)

RGN – Registered General Nurse (see also RNA)

Rh – rhesus factor (positive/negative for the D antigen in blood)

RHS – right-hand side

RICE – rest, ice, compression and elevation (soft tissue injury)

RICP – raised intracranial pressure (raised BP in the skull)

RIF – right iliac fossa (right side of the abdomen in the region of the appendix)

RIG – radiology inserted gastronomy (PEG guided by an X-ray)

RIH – right inguinal hernia (see LIH)

RIP – rest in peace (deceased)

RLT – model Roper, Logan and Tierney model of nursing

RMN – Registered Mental Nurse

RNA – 1. Registered Nurse Adult (RGN); 2. ribonucleic acid

RNIB – Royal National Institute of Blind People

RNMH – Registered Nurse Mental Health

RNP – Registered Nurse Practitioner

RNSC – Registered Nurse Sick Children

ROC – removal of clips

ROM – range of movement

ROS – removal of sutures

rpt – repeat

RR – respiratory rate (breaths per minute)

RSCN – Registered Sick Children's Nurse

RSD – reflex sympathetic dystrophy (chronic pain condition)

RSI – repetitive strain injury

Rt – right (write out in full)

RT – radiotherapy

RTA – road traffic accident

RTH – ready to hang bottle

RTS – raised toilet seat

RTW – returned to ward

Rv. – review

RVF – right ventricular failure

Rx – treatmenet

s – second (unit of time)

SA node – sinoatrial node (the heart's pacemaker cells)

SAD – seasonal affective disorder (the 'winter blues' brought on by a lack of sunlight; treated with light therapy)

SALT – speech and language therapist

SaO_2 – oxygen saturation (% oxygen in blood; pulse oximetry)

SAP – single assessment process

SARA – sexually acquired reactive arthritis

SARS – severe acute respiratory syndrome (the SARS virus)

SATS – (see SaO_2)

S/B – seen by

SBAR – situation, background, assessment, recommendation

s/c – subcutaneous (under the skin; into the adipose tissue)

SCBU – Special Care Baby Unit

SCC – 1. squameous cell carcinoma; 2. spinal cord compression

SCI – spinal cord injury

SDH – subdural haematoma (blood clot between brain and skull)

sec – second (also s)

SHO – senior house officer (a doctor training to be a registrar)

SI – International System of Units (metric units)

SIRS – systemic inflammatory response syndrome (a major inflammatory response following infection, sepsis, trauma, etc)

SL – sublingual (under the tongue)

SMI – silent myocardial ischaemia (eg a lack of angina pain in people with diabetes)

S/M – staff midwife

S/N – staff nurse

SOB – shortness of breath (dyspnoea; eg in COPD)

SOBAR – shortness of breath at rest

SOBOE – shortness of breath on exertion

SPR – specialist registrar (a doctor training in a speciality)

SR – sister

S/R – slow release (medication)

SSRI – selective serotonin reuptake inhibitor (antidepressants)

ST segment – part of an ECG after the QRS complex, before the T wave, that corresponds with contraction of the ventricles

STAT – given immediately as a single dose

STD – sexually transmitted disease

STEMI – ST segment elevation MI (as seen on an ECG)

ST/M – student midwife

STM – short-term memory

ST/N – student nurse

SVG – saphenous vein graft (see also CABG)

SVT – supraventricular tachycardia (a rapid heart rate (>100 bpm) that originated above the ventricles in the atria)

SW – social worker

SWL – safe working load (hoists)

Sx – 1. symptoms; 2. seizure

T – 1. thoracic vertebrae (T1 to T12); 2. temperature (low-grade pyrexia = 37.5–38.2 °C; medium = 38.3–39.7; high > 39.8)

T_4 – thyroxine (thyroid gland hormone; eg wt. gain if low)

TA – temporal arteritis (see GCA)

Tarde – in the evening (Latin)

TB – tuberculosis

TBI – traumatic brain injury

TC'd – treatment completed

TCI – patient to come in (a planned admission)

t.d.s. – three times daily (Latin)

TCOM – transcutanous oxygen monitoring

TDD – total daily dose

TED's – thrombo embolic deterrents (stockings used in the prophylaxis of VTE's)

Temp – temperature

TENS – transcutaneous electrical nerve stimulation (pain relief)

TFTs – thyroid function blood tests (venepuncture)

TGA – transient global anaemia (temporary memory loss)

THR – total hip replacement

TIA – transient ischaemic attack (a mini stroke)

t.i.d – see t.d.s

tinct – tincture (a medication that is dissolved in alcohol)

TKR – total knee replacement

TLC – 1. total lung capacity; 2. tender loving care – treat only with symptom relief and nursing care

TNF – tumour necrosis factor (causes joint damage in RA)

TNK – tenecteplase. A thrombolytic agent used to treat MI's

TnT – Troponin T. Cardiac enzyme measured after an MI; levels rise with heart muscle damage)

TOC – transfer of care

TOD – transfer of drug

TOE – transoesophageal echo (an echocardiogram with the scope passed down the oesophagus)

Top – topical (applied to the skin or other body surface)

TPN – total parenteral nutrition (intravenous feeding)

TPR – temperature pulse respiration (eg vital signs TPR chart)

Trigs. – triglycerides (fats in meat and diary products; lipids)

Trop T – see TnT

TSH – thyroid stimulating hormone (pituitary gland; blood test)

TTE – Transthoracic echo (ultrasound imaging of the heart)

TTOs/TTAs – discharge medications for patients to take out/away/home, on leaving hospital

TTR – target therapeutic range (eg as per INR)

TURP – transurethral resection of the prostate

TVN – tissue viability nurse (nurse specializing in wound care)

TWOC – trial without catheter. The indwelling catheter is removed to see if the patient can pass urine without it

Tx – 1. transfer; 2. treatment; 3. transplant

U – units

UA – urinalysis (urine tests)

UBW – usual body weight

U&Es – urea and electrolytes (a blood test)

UL – upper limit

UO – urinary output

URTI – upper respiratory tract infection (ie chest and head)

USA – under spinal anaesthesia

USS – ultrasound scan

UTI – urinary tract infection (eg urethra, bladder and ureters)

UV – ultraviolet (see also PUVA)

VAC – 1. vacuum-assisted closure (of a wound); 2. vaccination

VAD – ventricular assistance device (pump to support the heart)

Vag – vaginal

VB – venous bloods (blood taken from the veins for tests)

VC – vital capacity (the maximum amount of air that can be expelled from the lungs after taking the deepest breath)

VD – a sexually transmitted disease (STD)

VF – ventricular fibrillation (a cardiac arrest where the ventricles of the heart lose their rhythm and flutter)

VQ – scan ventilation/perfusion scan used to detect a PE

V/S – vital signs (key indicators of health including temperature, blood pressure, pulse, respirations and saturated oxygen levels (pulse oximetry; aka 'baseline observations', they can also include pain and neurological observations)

VT – ventricular tachycardia (a pulse rate of more than 100 bpm)

VTE – venous thromboembolism (a DVT or PE)

VZV – varicella zoster virus (causes chickenpox; shingles)

WBC – white blood cell count (also WCC white cell count) – (a blood test that is a marker for inflammation)

WHO – World Health Organization

W/O – without

Wt – weight

w/v – weight volume (concentration in grams per 100 ml)

X-MATCH – cross-match (blood group tested for compatibility; A, B, AB, or O)

XR – extended release (long-acting medications/capsules)

XRT – radiotherapy (an X-ray beam kills cancer cells)

y, yr – year

y/o – years old

ZF – Zimmer frame

Zn – the chemical symbol for zin

Alphabetical list of drugs named in the book

Selected brand names are shown with some typical indications.

A

acyclovir (Zovirax®) – for herpes infections; shingles
adrenaline (epinephrine) – for anaphylaxis (EpiPen®); CPR
alendronic acid (Fosamax®) – for osteoporosis
alfacalcidol (One-Alpha®) – for rickets; vitamin D deficiency
alfuzosin hydrochloride (Xatral®) – for urinary retention (men)
allopurinol (Zyloric®) – for gout
aminophylline – for asthma and COPD
amiodarone – for heart arrythmias (SVT, AF, VF)
amisulpride (Solian®) – for psychoses (schizophrenia)
amitriptyline – for neuropathic pain
amoxicillin – for bacterial infections
atenolol – for hypertension (beta-blocker)
atrovastatin (Lipitor®) – for lowering LDL cholesterol

B

baclofen (Lioresal®) – for spasticity in MS
betahistine (Serc®) – for vertigo
bisocodyl (Dulolax®) – laxative for constipation
bisoprolol (Cardicor®) – for hypertension (beta-blocker)
budesonide (Pulmicort®) – asthma
bumetanide – for oedema (loop diuretic)
bupivaciane (Marcain®) – for local anaesthesia

C

carbamazepine (Tegretol®) – for control of epilepsy (seizures)
carvedilol – for hypertension (beta-blocker)
cefalexin (Ceporex®; Keflex®; Tenkorex®) – for infections
cefotaxime – for bacterial infections, eg meningitis
ceftriaxone (Rocephin®) – for bacterial infections, eg respiratory
chlordiazepoxide (Librium®) – for anxiety; alcohol withdrawal
chlorphenamine (Piriton®) – for hay fever; a rash; anaphylaxis
ciprofloxacin (Ciproxin®) – for bacterial infections eg UTI
citalopram (Cipramil®) – for depression
clarithromycin (Klaricid®) – for bacterial infections, eg cellulitis
clopidrogel (Plavix®) – for prevention of blood clots
co-amoxiclav(Augmentin®) – for infections; contains amoxicillin
co-beneldopa (Madopar®) – for PD
co-careldopa (Sinemet®) – for PD
co-codamol (Kapake®; co-codamol 30/500) – for pain relief
colloid (Gelofusine®) – for increasing the blood volume
co-trimoxazole – for bacterial infections (contains trimethoprim)
cyclizine (Valoid®) – for N&V; motion sickness; vertigo

D

danaparoid sodium (Orgaran®) – for prevention of DVTs
darbepoetin alfa (Aranesp®) – erythropoietin – for anaemia
dexamethasone (dex) – for inflammatory and allergic disorders for
    nausea and vomiting in chemotherapy
dextrose 5% w/v; 50% w/v – see glucose
diamorphine (heroin) – for severe pain
diazepam (Valium®) – for anxiety; insomnia; convulsions
diclofenac (Voltarol®) – NSAID for rheumatoid arthritis

digoxin (Lanoxin-PG®) – for AF (not if rest pulse < 60 bpm)
dipyridamole (Persantin®; Persantin® Retard) – for prevention of
    blood clots; modified release prevents ischemic stroke, TIAs)
disodium etidronate (Didronel®) – for osteoporosis
disulfiram (Antabuse®) – for alcohol abuse
dobutamine – for cardiogenic shock; septic shock
domperidone (Motilium®) – for nausea and vomiting
donepezil (Aricept®) – for Alzheimer's disease (dementia)
dopamine (Intropin®) – for cardiogenic shock

E

enoxaparin (Clexane®) – for anticoagulation (DVT, PE)
entanercept (Enbrel®) – for RA
epinephrine (see adrenaline)
erythromycin – for infections when allergic to penicillin
etoricoxib (Arcoxia®) – for OA and RA

F

fentanyl transdermal patch (Durogesic®) – for pain relief
flecainide (Tambacor®) – for heart arrhythmias (eg AF)
flucloxacillin – for bacterial infections (antibiotic)
fluoxetine (Prozac®) – for depression
furosemide or frusemide (Frusol®; Lasix®) – for oedema

G

gentamycin (Viaflex® bag) – for septicaemia; pneumonia
gliclazide – for type 2 diabetes
glucose 5% infusion fluid – for fluid replacement
glucose 50% IV bolus dose – for hypoglycaemia
glycereol suppositories – for constipation
glyceryl trinitrate (GTN) aerosol (Nitrolingual®) – for angina

H

haloperidol (Serenace®; Haldol®;) – delusions; hallucinations
heparin (Hepsal®) – for the prevention of blood clots
hyoscine butyl-bromide (Buscopan®) – for excess secretions; IBS
hyoscine hydro-bromide (Kwells®) – for motion sickness

I

ibuprofen (Brufen®) – NSAID for pain relief (arthritis)
imipenem with cilastatin (Primaxin®) – for infections
insulin glargine (Lantus®) – for type 1 and type 2 diabetes
ipratropium bromide (Atrovent®) – for COPD

K

ketamine – for anaesthesia and analgesia

L

lactulose – for relief of constipation; hepatic encephalopathy
lansoprazole (Zoton®) – for reducing gastic acid (antacid)
lercanidipine (Zanidip®) – for hypertension
levomepromazine (Nozinan®) – for restlessness and agitation
levothyroxine – for low thyroid hormone; myxodema
lidocaine (lignocaine) – for local anaesthesia; ventricular
    arrhythmias following MI
lithium citrate – for bipolar disorder

M

meloxicam (Mobic®) – for RA; OA exacerbation
metaclopramide (Maxolon®) – for nausea and vomiting
metformin – for type 2 diabetes (a gold standard treatment)
metrondiazole (Flagyl®) – for bacterial infections (eg C diff)
midazolam (Hypnovel®) – for sedation
mirtazapine (Zispin®) – for clinical depression
morphine (sulphate oral solution – Oromorph®) – for pain relief
morphine (sulphate tablets – MST – Sevredol®) – for pain relief
mupirocin (topical cream; Bactroban®) – for nasal MRSA

N

N-acetylcysteine (Parvolex®) – for paracetamol overdose
naloxone (Narcan®) – for reversal of opiod overdose
nicorandil (Ikorel®) – for angina
nifedipine (Adalat®) – for angina
nystatin (Nystan®) – for fungal infections

O

omeprazole (Losec®) – for or to prevent gastric ulcers
oral morphine (Oramorph®) – see morphine

P

pancreatin (Creon®) – for pancreatic enzyme deficiency
pantoprazole (Protium®) – for or to prevent gastric ulcers
paracetamol (Calpol®; Panadol®) – for pain relief and pyrexia
perindropril (Coversyl®) – for hypertension; heart failure; CCB
pethidine – for pain relief (pca pump)
phenobarbital elixir – for control of epileptic seizures
phenytoin (Epanutin®) – for control of epileptic seizures
potassium chloride (Sando-K®) – for low potassium
pramipexole (Mirapexin®) – for PD; restless legs syndrome
procainamide – for heart arrhythmias

Q

quetiapine (Seroquel®) – for mania; hallucinations
quinine – for leg cramps; also malaria

R

ranitidine (Zantac®) – for heartburn and indigestion
risedronate (Actonel®) – for osteoporosis
rivastigmine (Exelon®) – for dementia
ropinirole (Requip®) – for PD; restless legs syndrome
rosiglitazone (Avandia®) – for diabetes

S

salbutamol (Ventolin®) – for COPD
salmeterol (Serevent®) – for asthma
senna (Senokot®) – for constipation
silver sulfadiazine (Flamazine®) – for burn wounds; leg ulcers
simvastatin – for lowering LDL cholesterol
sodium chloride 0.9 % ('normal saline') – for infusions
sodium nitroprusside – for acute hypertension
sodium valproate (Epilim®) – for control of epilepsy
sulindac (Clinoril®) – for rheumatoid arthritis

T

tamsulosin (Flomax®) – for urinary retention (prostate)

temazepam – for insomnia; mild sedation with amnesia

terbutaline (Bricanyl®) – for asthma

tiotropium bromide (Spiriva®) – for COPD

tolterodine (Detrusitol®) – for incontinence (frequency, urgency)

trazodone (Molpaxin®) – for depression and anxiety

trimethoprim – for bacterial infections, eg UTI, respiratory tract

V

valproate (see sodium valproate)

vancomycin – for C-diff and MRSA infections

verapamil (Securon®) – for hypertension; angina (CCB)

vitamin B and C injection (Pabrinex®) – for deficiencies in these
vitamins (eg caused by alcoholism)

W

warfarin – for anticoagulation (prevents blood clot)

Z

zinc and castor oil – for urinary rash

zopiclone (Zimovane®) – for insomnia

Alphabetical list of drug brand names

A

Actonel® (risedonate); Actrapid® (human insulin); Adalat® (nifedpine); Antabuse® (disulfiram); Aransep® (darbepoetin alfa); Arcoxia® (etoricoxib); Aricept® (donepezil); Atrovent® (ipratopium bromide); Augmentin® (co-amoxiclav); Avandia® (rosiglitazone)

B

Baclofen® (lioresal); Bactroban® (2% w/w mupirocin); Bricanyl (terbutaline sulphate); Brufen® (ibuprofen); Buscopan® (hyoscine butyl-bromide)

C

Calpol® (paracetamol); Cardicor® (bisoprolol); Ceporex® (cefalexin); Cipramil® (citalopram); Ciproxin® (ciprofloxacin); Clexane® (enoxoparin); Clinoril® (sulindac); Combinvent (ipratopium bromide and salbutamol); Coversyl® (perindopril); Creon® (pancreatin)

D

Detrusitol® (tolterodine); Didronel (disodium etidronate);
Dulcolax® (bisocodyl); Durogesic® (fentanly patch)

E

Enbrel® (etanercept); Epanutin® (phenytoin); Epilim®
(sodium valproate); EpiPen® (adrenaline); Exelon® (rivastigmine)

F

Flagyl® (metrondiazole); Flamazine® (silver sulphadiazine);
Flomax® (tamsulosin); Fosamax® (aldronic acid);
Frusol® (frusemide)

G

Gelofusine® (colloid)

H

Hepsal® (heparin); Humulin® (synthetic human insulin);
Hypnovel® (midazolam)

I

Ikorel® (nicorandil); Inatropin® (dopamine)

J

Jevity® (nutritional feed via a tube)

K

Kapake® (30/500 co-codamol); Keflex® (cefalexin);
Klaricid® (clarithromycin); Kwells® (hyosciene hydro-bromide)

L

Lantus® (insulin glargine); Lanoxin-PG® (digoxin);
Lasix® (furosemide); Librium® (chloradiazopoxide);
Lipitor® (atrovastatin); Losec® (omeprazole)

M

Madopar® (co-beneldopa); Marcaine® (bupivacaine); Maxolon® (metoclopramide); Mirapexine® (pramipexole); Mixtard® (biphasic insulin); Molipaxin® (trazodone); Motilium® (domeridone)

N

Narcan® (naxolone); Nozinan® (levomepromazine); Nitrolingual® pump spray (GTN); Nystan® (nystatin)

O

One-Alpha® (alfacalcidol); Oramorph® (morphine oral solution); Orgaran® (danaporoid sodium)

P

Pabrinex® (vitamin B and C injection); Panadol® (paracetamol); Parvolex® (N-acetylcysteine); Persantin® (dipyridamole); Piroton® (chlorphenamine); Plavix® (clopidrogel); Primaxin® (imipenem with cilastin); Protium® (pantoprazole); Prozac® (fluoxetine); Pulmicort® (budesonide)

R

Requip® (ropinirole); Rocephin® (ceftriaxone)

S

Sando-K® (potassium chloride); Securon® (verapamil hydrochloride); Senokot® (senna); Serc® (betahistine); Serenace® (haloperidol); Serevent® (salmetrol); Seroquel® (quetiapine); Sevredol® (MST); Sinemet® (co-careldopa); Slow-K® (potassium chloride); Solian® (amisulpride); Solpadol® (30/500 co-codamol); Spiriva® (tiotropium bromide); Symbicort® (budensonide + formoterol)

T

Tambaco® (flecainide); Tegretol® (carbemazapine); Tylex® (30/500 co-codamol)

V

Valium® (diazepam); Valoid® (cyclizine); Ventolin® (salbutamol); Viaflex® (gentamycin); Voltarol® (diclofenac)

X

Xatral® (alfuzosin hydrochloride)

Z

Zanidip® (lercanidipine); Zantac® (ranitidine); Zapain® (30/500 co-codamol); Zimovane® (zopiclone); Zispin® (mirtazapine); Zoton® (lanzoprazole); Zovirax® (acyclovir); Zyloric® (allopurinol)

Further reading from Kogan Page

- *Essay Writing Skills*   978 0 7494 6391 5
- *How to Get into Medical School*   978 0 7494 6140 9
- *How to Master the BMAT*, 2nd edition   978 0 7494 6336 6
- *How to Master the UKCAT*, 4th edition   978 0 7494 6821 7
- *How to Pass Advanced Numeracy Tests*   978 0 7494 6789 0
- *How to Pass Numeracy Tests*   978 0 7494 6791 3
- *How to Pass Numerical Reasoning Tests*   978 0 7494 6797 5
- *The Study Skills Guide*   978 0 7494 6126 3